i n s p i r e

NANCY DOUGLAS

ANDREW BOON

 **NATIONAL GEOGRAPHIC LEARNING** |  **CENGAGE Learning**

Australia • Brazil • Japan • Korea • Mexico • Singapore • Spain • United Kingdom • United States

P9-EJU-650

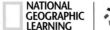 

Inspire 3
Nancy Douglas and Andrew Boon

Publisher: Andrew Robinson

Executive Editor: Sean Bermingham

Senior Development Editor: Derek Mackrell

Editorial Assistant: Dylan Mitchell

Director of Global Marketing: Ian Martin

Senior Product Marketing Manager:
Caitlin Thomas

Senior Director of Production:
Michael Burggren

Senior Content Project Manager: Tan Jin Hock

Manufacturing Planner: Mary Beth Hennebury

Compositor: Page 2, LLC.

Cover/Text Design: Creative Director:
Christopher Roy, Art Director: Scott Baker,
Designer: Alex Dull

Cover Photos: (front) Paul Nicklen/National
Geographic Creative, (back) Pablo Hidalgo/
Shutterstock.com

ISBN-13: 978-1-133-96342-4

ISBN-10: 1-133-96342-0

National Geographic Learning
20 Channel Center Street
Boston, MA 02210
USA

Cengage Learning is a leading provider of customized learning solutions with office locations around the globe, including Singapore, the United Kingdom, Australia, Mexico, Brazil, and Japan. Locate your local office at:
international.cengage.com/region

Cengage Learning products are represented in Canada by Nelson Education, Ltd.

Visit National Geographic Learning online at **NGL.Cengage.com**

Visit our corporate website at **www.cengage.com**

Printed in the United States
4 5 6 7 — 18 17 16 15

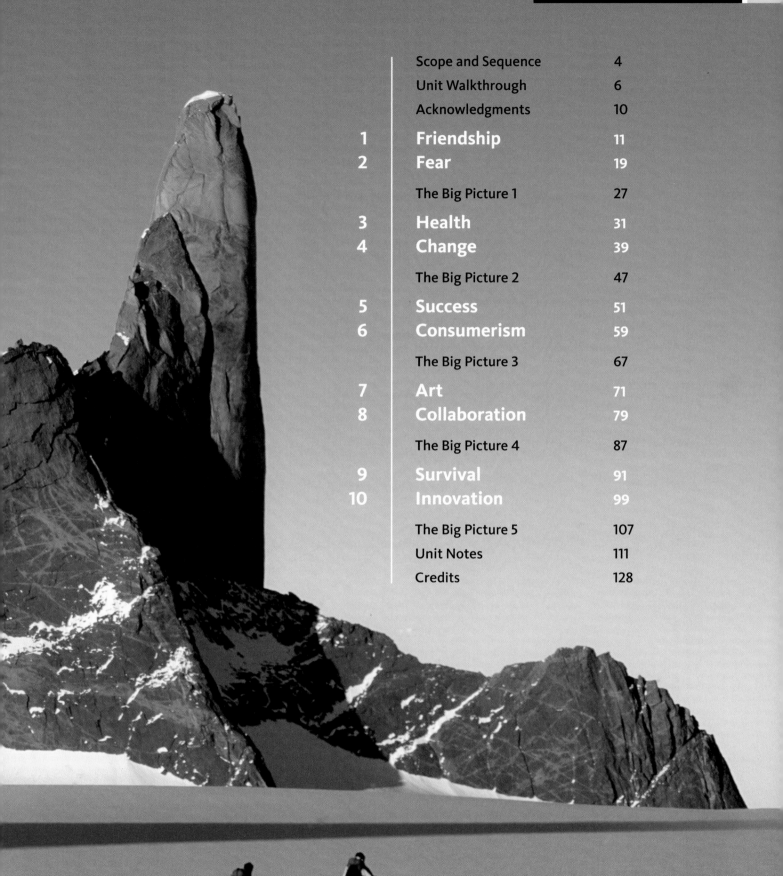

Contents

Scope and Sequence

Unit Walkthrough

Unit Opener

Warm Up discussion questions introduce the unit topic.

Lesson A

Listening sections gradually progress from closed listening tasks to open discussion, providing the scaffolding students need.

Conversation sections provide both guided and personalized conversation practice.

Audio icons indicate CD and audio track numbers.

Listening activities practice a range of listening skills.

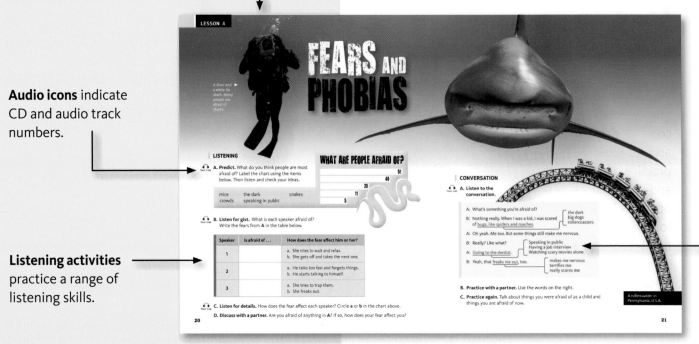

Lesson B

Reading passages are adapted and graded from authentic sources. They provide content input to act as a stimulus for discussion later in this section.

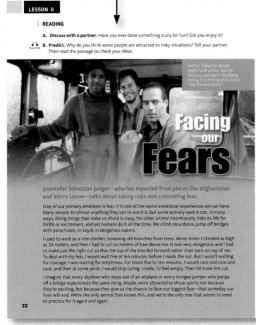

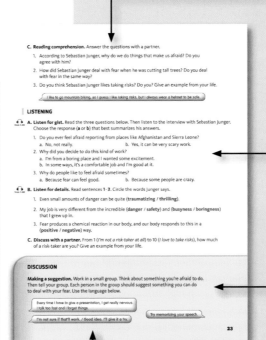

Reading comprehension questions check students' understanding of the reading passage.

A second **listening section** provides additional listening practice and further develops the ideas introduced in the reading passage.

Discussion sections introduce and practice functional language and expressions.

In some units, **split activities** indicate in **red** where one student turns to the end of the book.

Language models in speech bubbles provide examples.

Video

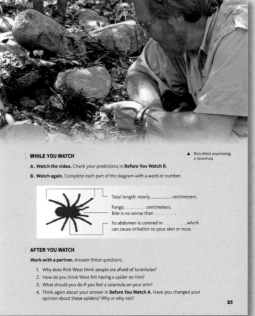

Video activities give extra comprehension and vocabulary practice, and provide opportunities for authentic input, acting as a springboard for discussion.

Unit Walkthrough

Expansion Activity

Expansion activities encourage students to use the language they've encountered in the unit and extend themselves in freer practice.

Tip boxes provide suggestions for ways students can use technology, such as cell phones, to assist them.

Unit Notes

Unit notes at the back of the book provide additional material for split activities, as well as language notes, and suggestions for additional activities.

Target vocabulary provides definitions for key topic related vocabulary from the unit.

Important language gives a summary of language structures from the unit.

Project ideas usually build upon the Expansion Activity, and provide suggestions for ways in which students can take their learning beyond the classroom.

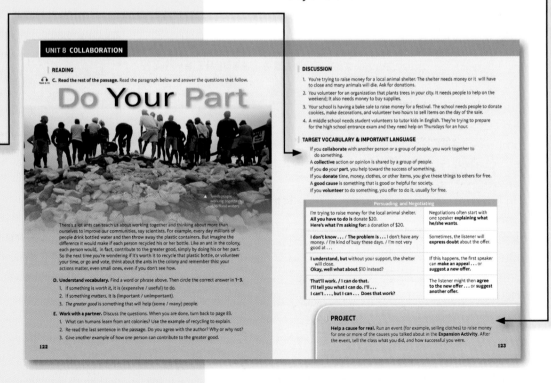

The Big Picture

There are five Big Picture sections, one after every two units. These sections review the previous two units and allow further opportunities for discussion.

Observation and discussion activities use the large photo to encourage communication and language practice.

Caption competition encourages students to think creatively about the image.

A stunning photo acts as a motivating prompt for discussion.

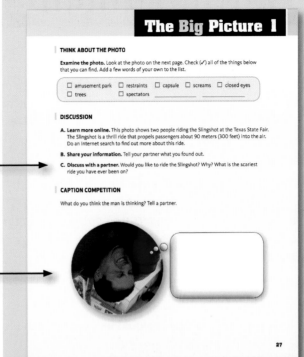

Review activities recycle and practice key language and vocabulary from the previous two units.

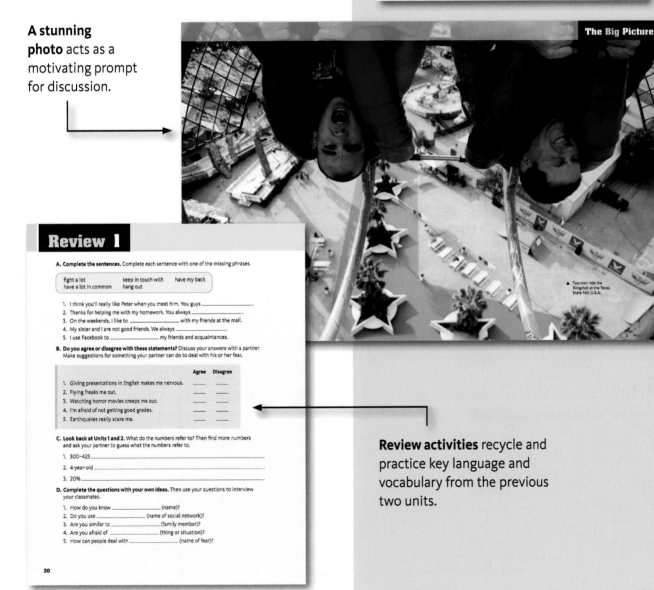

▲ Two men ride the Slingshot at the Texas State Fair, U.S.A.

Acknowledgments

I would like to thank everyone who participated in the development of this series. Special thanks go to publisher Andrew Robinson for inviting me to be a part of this project, to Derek Mackrell for his editorial expertise and encouragement, and to Andy Boon for his invaluable support and inspiration. I am also grateful to my husband Jorge and daughter Jasmine for the love and encouragement they provided during the writing of this book.

Nancy Douglas

I would like to thank my wonderful co-author and editorial team for their enthusiasm, ideas, and work throughout the Inspire project. I would also like to thank all the students I have ever taught—you guys ARE the inspiration!

Andrew Boon

The Authors and Publishers would like to thank the following teaching professionals for their valuable feedback during the development of this series.

Jennifer Alicea, UPR Ponce, Puerto Rico, United States; **Grace Bishop**, Houston Community College, Houston, United States; **Leonardo Escobar**, Universidad Manuela Beltra, Bogotá, Colombia; **David Fairweather**, Asahikawa Medical University, Hokkaido, Japan; **Wendy M. Gough**, St. Mary College/Nunoike Gaigo Senmon Gakko, Nagoya, Japan; **Erica Harris**, Lewis & Clark College, Portland, United States; **Ikuko Kashiwabara**, Osaka Electro-Communication University, Neyagawa, Japan; **Maureen Kelbert**, Vancouver Community College, Vancouver, Canada; **Jungryul Kim**, Korea National University of Education, Cheongwon, South Korea; **Bridget McDonald**, ELC Boston, Boston, United States; **Jill McDonough**, South Seattle Community College, Seattle, United States; **Kent McLeod**, UT Arlington English Language Institute, Mansfield, United States; **Donna Moore**, Hawaii Community College, Hilo, United States; **Nancy Nystrom**, University of Texas at San Antonio, San Antonio, United States; **Jane O'Connor**, Emory College of Arts and Sciences, Decatur, United States; **Elizabeth Ortiz**, COPEI-COPOL English Institute, Guayaquil, Ecuador; **Maeran Park**, Bukyoung National University, Busan, South Korea; **Terri Rapoport**, ELS Educational Services, Inc., Princeton, United States; **Amy Renehan**, University of Washington, Seattle, United States; **Greg Rouault**, Konan University, Hirao School of Management, Nishinomiya, Japan; **Elena Sapp**, INTO Oregon State University, Corvallis, United States; **Anne-Marie Schlender**, Austin Community College, Austin, United States; **Karen Shock**, Savannah College of Art and Design, Atlanta, United States; **Julie Thornton**, CSULB American Language Institute, Santa Ana, United States; **Rosa E. Vasquez Fernandez**, John F. Kennedy Institute of Languages, Inc., STI, Dominican Republic; **Matthew Walters**, Hongik University, Seoul, South Korea; **Christie Ward**, Central Connecticut State University, New Britain, United States; **Matthew Watterson**, Hongik University, Mapo-Gu, South Korea; **Chris Willson**, Meio University, Okinawa, Japan; **Kyungsook Yeum**, Sookmyung Women's University, Seoul, South Korea

Friendship

Piek, a four-year-old monkey, and one-year-old Pom live in Ayutthaya, Thailand. The animals were left by their owners and take care of each other.

WARM UP

Answer these questions with a partner.

1. Do you think it's easy or difficult to make new friends? Why?
2. Have you made any friends online?
3. Do you prefer to have lots of acquaintances or a few close friends?

Your Social Network

World Map of Social Networks, 2013

Over a billion people worldwide connect with friends using social networking websites.

LISTENING

A. Discuss with a partner. Look at the map. Answer the questions.

1. Worldwide, which website is the most popular? Which is the most popular in your country?
2. Do you use any of the sites in the chart? If so, which ones?

Track 1-01

B. Listen for gist. *the big idea not details.* Read the four questions below. Can you guess any of the answers? Then listen and number the questions (**1–4**) in the order the woman answers them. You will hear only the woman's answers, not the questions.

_2_ Who are most teenagers friends with on Facebook?	1. ___300___ to ___425___	
_3_ Is it common for teens to accept *usual* friend requests from strangers?	2. _classmates_, _family_ members, and _close_ friends	
_1_ How many friends do most teens have on Facebook?	3. _yes_. In fact, they don't know ___25___% of their online friends.	
_4_ What do teens like about Facebook?	4. connecting with _friends_ *but peer pressure is a problem* *equal to something.*	

Track 1-01

C. Listen for details. Listen again and complete the answers to **1–4** in **B**. Write a word or number in each space.

D. Discuss with a partner. How do you feel about sites like Facebook? Are any of the answers above true for you?

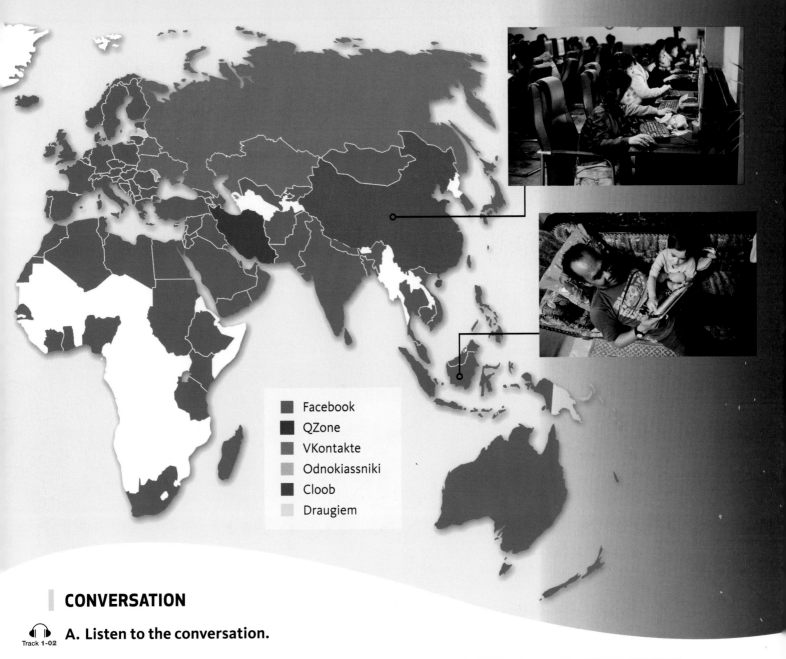

Legend:
- Facebook
- QZone
- VKontakte
- Odnokiassniki
- Cloob
- Draugiem

CONVERSATION

A. Listen to the conversation.

Track 1-02

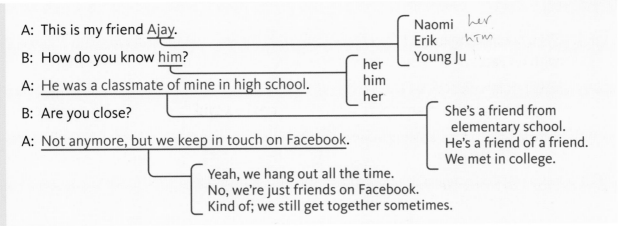

A: This is my friend Ajay.

B: How do you know him?

A: He was a classmate of mine in high school.

B: Are you close?

A: Not anymore, but we keep in touch on Facebook.

Naomi   her
Erik   him
Young Ju

her
him
her

She's a friend from elementary school.
He's a friend of a friend.
We met in college.

Yeah, we hang out all the time.
No, we're just friends on Facebook.
Kind of; we still get together sometimes.

B. Practice with a partner. Use the words on the right.

C. Practice again. Talk about friends of yours. Explain how you know each person. Use your phone to show photos of your friends to your partner.

▲ Players from different ice hockey teams in Plaster Rock, Canada

READING

A. Predict. Read the first sentence of the passage. How would you answer this question? Make a list of your ideas.

Track 1-03 **B. Read the passage.** As you read, underline the reasons we choose our friends.

You've Got to Have Friends

We all know that having friends is important, but why do we form friendships with some people and not others? In some ways, the answer is simple: you become friends with someone because you have things in common. Maybe you both like the same soccer team. Or perhaps you both love to play video games. Or maybe your personalities are similar: you're a bit shy and the other person is, too.

But two American scientists, Peter DeScioli and Robert Kurzban, found that we form friendships with certain people for another reason: because these relationships protect us in some way. Their research also showed that we rank our friends on how likely they are to "have our back"—that is, to support us when there is trouble. The more likely a person is to help you, the closer a friend he or she is. For this reason, it's possible to be friends with someone who is different from you. You get along because the person can help you in some way, the researchers say, and that's even more important than your differences.

C. Reading comprehension. For each sentence, circle the correct answers.

1. Peter DeScioli and Robert Kurzban believe . . .

   a. most people are friends because they are similar in some way.
   (b) our closest friends are the ones who help us when there is a problem.
   c. it's uncommon to be friends with people who are different from you. *larity*

2. Something you *have in common* with someone is a (**difference** / **similarity**) between you.

3. If a friend *has your back*, *take care.* he or she (**helps** / **doesn't help**) you when there is a problem.

4. If you *get along* with someone, you (**are** / **aren't**) friendly with him or her.
   have a good relationship with them

D. Discuss with a partner. Think of one of your friends. Are you friends with this person for any of the reasons mentioned in the reading?

LISTENING

Track 1-04
A. Listen for gist. Listen and choose the correct answer. What is the book the speaker is discussing mainly about?

   a. how to be a good friend   c. how our friendships are different
   b. why some friendships end   (d.) ways to make friends with new people

Track 1-04
B. Listen for details. Match a type of friend (**1–4**) with the correct description (**a–d**).

1. The Companion *best friend*   a. always puts you in a good mood.
2. The Collaborator *have common* b. is the friend you have the most in common with.
3. The Energizer   c. is the friend you're most likely to learn new things from.
4. The Mind-Opener   d. is the friend you're most likely to share a secret with.

C. Discuss with a partner. Think about one of your friends. What kind of friend (**1–4**) is he or she to you? What kind of friend are you to him or her? Why?

DISCUSSION

Describing similarities and differences. What are your friends like? Are they similar to or different from you? How? Tell a partner using the language below and on page 111.

> My best friend Jin and I have a lot in common. / are kind of similar. / are completely different.

UNLIKELY FRIENDS

◀ Koza and Cairo in San Diego Zoo, U.S.A.

BEFORE YOU WATCH

About the video. At the San Diego Zoo in the U.S., a lion cub (a young lion) named Koza is friends with a puppy (a young dog) named Cairo. Normally, dogs and large **predators**, like lions, aren't **compatible**, but at the zoo, the pair are friends.

eat other thing   *get along / friend*

A. Vocabulary definitions. Circle the correct word(s) to complete each definition below.

1. If two people or animals are *compatible*, they (get along well / fight a lot).

2. A *predator* is an animal that (eats / is eaten by) other animals.

B. Predict. Guess the answer to the questions. Share your ideas with a partner.

1. Why do you think Koza and Cairo became friends?

    _____

2. Do you think they will still be friends when they are fully grown?

    _____

WHILE YOU WATCH

A. Check your answers. As you watch, check your answers in **Before You Watch**.

B. Watch again. Are the statements below **True** or **False**?

	True	False
1. Many animals are social in the wild. *(nature)*	✓	
2. San Diego Zoo rarely puts animals of different species together.	✓	✓
3. Today, Majani the cheetah and Clifford the dog get along well.	✓	
4. Soon the zoo will have to separate Cairo and Koza.	✓	
5. A lot of cross-species friendships actually happen in the wild.		✓

AFTER YOU WATCH

A. Talk with a partner. How likely would you be to be friends with the people below? Give your opinion and explain your answer. Take turns. Which opinion (possible or difficult) is the most common?

It's (**possible / difficult**) to be friends with _____.

1. a member of the opposite sex
2. a person your parents' age
3. someone much richer or poorer than you
4. an ex-boyfriend or ex-girlfriend
5. a person from another country

B. Compare results. Compare your responses as a class.

> I think it's difficult to be friends with a person your parents' age. They're older and they have different interests.

A chimpanzee ▶
and a dog share
an embrace.

A FRIENDSHIP SURVEY

You are going to give a short presentation about friendship.

A. Work with a partner. Choose a topic from the box below.

How to . . .
• make a new friend from a different culture • be a good friend • get along with a difficult person • your idea _____

B. Survey your classmates. Ask them for suggestions on your topic. Then look at your results. Choose the most useful suggestions and add your own ideas.

C. Create a presentation. With your partner, create a presentation. You can create a poster, use slides, or make a video. See page 111 for examples of language you can use.

D. Work with another pair. Pair 1: Give your presentation. **Pair 2:** Listen and answer these questions: Are the ideas helpful? Which idea is the best? Is there anything else you'd suggest? Then swap.

> How can you make a friend from a different culture?

> Talk to them after class. Find out if you have anything in common.

Do an online search for "how people become friends." Use this information to help you write your extra question in **A**.

A group of friends ▼ having fun, Alaska, U.S.A.

Fear

Climber Alex Honnold walks along
a narrow ledge in Yosemite, U.S.A.

WARM UP

Answer these questions with a partner.

1. How do you think the man in the photo feels? How would you feel?

2. What are some things people are often afraid of?

3. When something scary happens, do you usually *freak out* or *stay calm*?

19

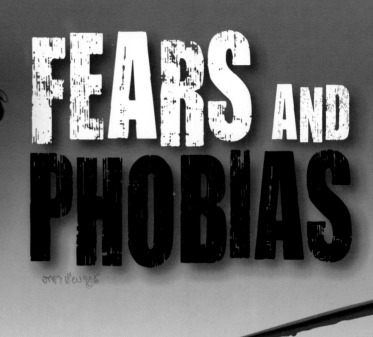

FEARS AND PHOBIAS

◀ A diver and a white tip shark. Many people are afraid of sharks.

LISTENING

Track 1-05

A. Predict. What do you think people are most afraid of? Label the chart using the items below. Then listen and check your ideas.

mice	the dark	snakes
crowds	speaking in public	

WHAT ARE PEOPLE AFRAID OF?

snakes	51
speaking in public	40
mice	20
crowds	11
the dark	5

Track 1-06

B. Listen for gist. What is each speaker afraid of? Write the fears from **A** in the table below.

Speaker	is afraid of . . .	How does the fear affect him or her?
1	Crowds public transportation	a. She tries to wait and relax. (b.) She gets off and takes the next one.
2	speak infront of class	(a.) He talks too fast and forgets things. b. He starts talking to himself.
3	mice	a. She tries to trap them. (b.) She freaks out.

Track 1-06
C. Listen for details. How does the fear affect each speaker? Circle **a** or **b** in the chart above.

D. Discuss with a partner. Are you afraid of anything in **A**? If so, how does your fear affect you?

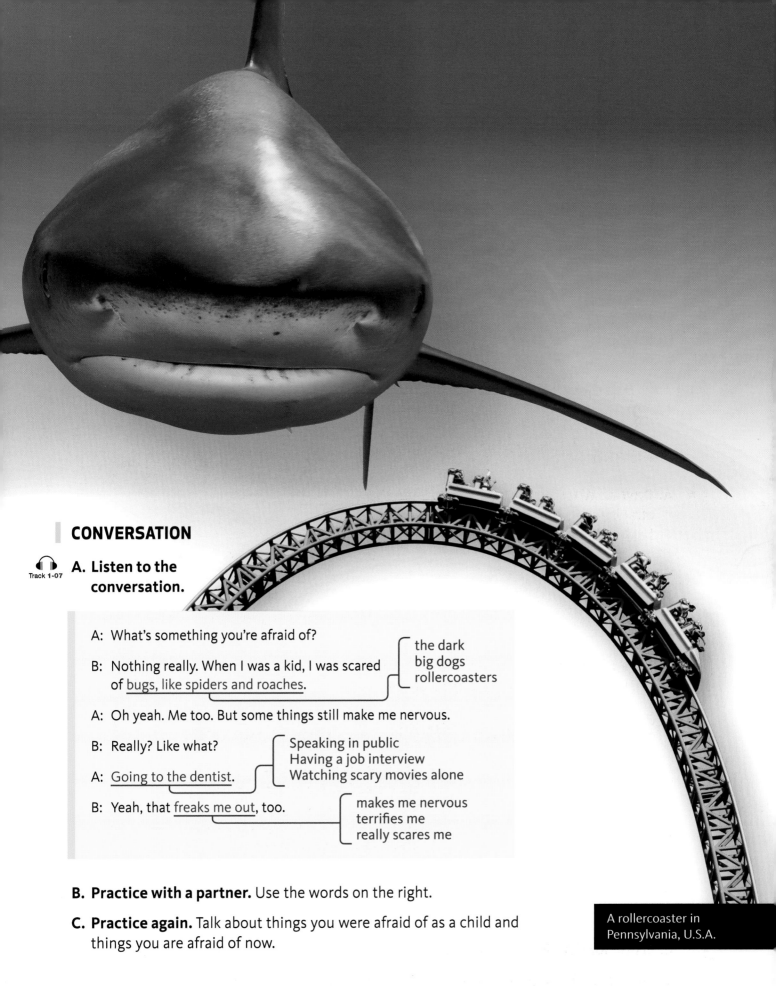

CONVERSATION

Track 1-07 **A. Listen to the conversation.**

A: What's something you're afraid of?

B: Nothing really. When I was a kid, I was scared of <u>bugs, like spiders and roaches</u>.

the dark
big dogs
rollercoasters

A: Oh yeah. Me too. But some things still make me nervous.

B: Really? Like what?

A: <u>Going to the dentist</u>.

Speaking in public
Having a job interview
Watching scary movies alone

B: Yeah, that <u>freaks me out</u>, too.

makes me nervous
terrifies me
really scares me

B. Practice with a partner. Use the words on the right.

C. Practice again. Talk about things you were afraid of as a child and things you are afraid of now.

A rollercoaster in Pennsylvania, U.S.A.

READING

A. Discuss with a partner. Have you ever done something scary for fun? Did you enjoy it?

Track 1-08

B. Predict. Why do you think some people are attracted to risky situations? Tell your partner. Then read the passage to check your ideas.

Author Sebastian Junger (right) with actors George Clooney and Mark Wahlberg during the filming of his book "The Perfect Storm."

Facing our Fears

Journalist Sebastian Junger—who has reported from places like Afghanistan and Sierra Leone—talks about taking risks and controlling fear.

One of our primary emotions is fear. It is one of the worst emotional experiences we can have. Many people do almost anything they can to avoid it, but some actively seek it out. In many ways, doing things that make us afraid is crazy. No other animal intentionally risks its life for thrills or excitement, and yet humans do it all the time. We climb mountains, jump off bridges with parachutes, or kayak in dangerous waters.

I used to work as a tree climber, removing old branches from trees. Many times I climbed as high as 24 meters, and then I had to cut six meters of tree above me. It was very dangerous and I had to make just the right cut so that the top of the tree fell forward rather than back on top of me. To deal with my fear, I would wait five or ten minutes before I made the cut. But I wasn't waiting for courage; I was waiting for emptiness. For those five to ten minutes, I would care and care and care, and then at some point, I would stop caring. Inside, I'd feel empty. Then I'd make the cut.

I imagine that every skydiver who steps out of an airplane or every bungee jumper who jumps off a bridge experiences the same thing. Maybe we're attracted to these sports not because they're exciting, but because they give us the chance to face our biggest fear—that someday our lives will end. We're the only animal that knows this, and we're the only one that seems to need to practice for it again and again.

C. Reading comprehension. Answer the questions with a partner.

1. According to Sebastian Junger, why do we do things that make us afraid? Do you agree with him? _to facing our fears_ _Yes_

2. How did Sebastian Junger deal with fear when he was cutting tall trees? Do you deal with fear in the same way? _Yes, stop caring and feel empty._

3. Do you think Sebastian Junger likes taking risks? Do you? Give an example from your life. _Yes. Sometime. I like to ride the high things._

> I like to go mountain biking, so I guess I like taking risks, but I always wear a helmet to be safe.

LISTENING

Track 1-09

A. Listen for gist. Read the three questions below. Then listen to the interview with Sebastian Junger. Choose the response (**a** or **b**) that best summarizes his answers.

1. Do you ever feel afraid reporting from places like Afghanistan and Sierra Leone?
   a. No, not really.   **b.** Yes, it can be very scary work.

2. Why did you decide to do this kind of work?
   a. I'm from a boring place and I wanted some excitement.
   b. In some ways, it's a comfortable job and I'm good at it.

3. Why do people like to feel afraid sometimes?
   a. Because fear can feel good.   b. Because some people are crazy.

Track 1-09

B. Listen for details. Read sentences **1–3**. Circle the words Junger says.

1. Even small amounts of danger can be quite (**traumatizing**/ **thrilling**).

2. My job is very different from the incredible (**danger** / **safety**) and (**busyness** / **boringness**) that I grew up in.

3. Fear produces a chemical reaction in our body, and our body responds to this in a (**positive**/ **negative**) way.

C. Discuss with a partner. From 1 (*I'm not a risk-taker at all*) to 10 (*I love to take risks*), how much of a risk-taker are you? Give an example from your life. ⑤

DISCUSSION

Making a suggestion. Work in a small group. Think about something you're afraid to do. Then tell your group. Each person in the group should suggest something you can do to deal with your fear. Use the language below.

> Every time I have to give a presentation, I get really nervous. I talk too fast and I forget things.

> Try memorizing your speech.

> I'm not sure if that'll work. / Good idea. I'll give it a try.

THE WORLD'S LARGEST SPIDER

▲ A goliath tarantula, the largest spider in the world— shown actual size.

BEFORE YOU WATCH

About the video. Tarantulas are a type of large spider that **creep** most people **out**. In the video, spider expert Rick West visits French Guiana in South America to find the goliath tarantula. He wants to teach people about this misunderstood **creature**.

A. Work with a partner. Read **About the video**, and make sure you understand the words in **bold**. Then check the sentence below that best describes your feelings about tarantulas. Explain your answer to a partner.

☐ I think tarantulas are cool creatures; I might get one for a pet.

☑ Tarantulas don't bother me, but I wouldn't want to touch one.

☐ Tarantulas creep me out!

B. Predict. What do you know about tarantulas? Choose **true** or **false**.

	True	False
1. Most tarantulas live mainly by eating small animals, like mice.	✓	
2. Most tarantulas live inside large trees.	✓	✓
3. You're most likely to see a tarantula in the daytime.		✓
4. A lot of people die each year from tarantula bites.		✓

WHILE YOU WATCH

A. Watch the video. Check your predictions in **Before You Watch B**.

B. Watch again. Complete each part of the diagram with a word or number.

Total length: nearly ___30___ centimeters.

Fangs: ___5___ centimeters.
Bite is no worse than a _bee sting_

Its abdomen is covered in _small hairs_ , which
can cause irritation to your skin or nose.

AFTER YOU WATCH

Work with a partner. Answer these questions.

1. Why does Rick West think people are afraid of tarantulas?
2. How do you think West felt having a spider on him?
3. What should you do if you feel a tarantula on your arm?
4. Think again about your answer in **Before You Watch A**. Have you changed your opinion about these spiders? Why or why not?

Scary Animals Presentation

You are going to give a presentation on a scary animal.

A. Work as a class. Make a list of animals that many people think are scary.

B. Work with a partner. Choose one animal from the list. Research it, answering the questions below. Find facts to help people understand this animal better.

- Where does the animal live?
- How big is it? Is it dangerous? If so, how?
- Why are many people afraid of it?
- Is there a good reason to be afraid of it?
- What things can people do to deal with their fear? Give at least two suggestions.

C. Create a presentation about your animal. Find a picture of it and a map or photo that shows where it lives.

D. Present your animal. Join two other pairs. Take turns giving your presentation. The group will listen and answer the five questions in **B** about your animal. Then, decide as a group: What was the scariest animal you learned about? Why?

Do an online search to see if some people keep your animal as a pet. Find out why they think it makes a good pet.

▲ The pit viper is a very dangerous snake that lives in Thailand.

THINK ABOUT THE PHOTO

Examine the photo. Look at the photo on the next page. Check (✓) all of the things below that you can find. Add a few words of your own to the list.

☑ amusement park ☑ restraints ☑ capsule ☑ screams ☑ closed eyes

☑ trees ☑ spectators _____ _____

DISCUSSION

A. **Learn more online.** This photo shows two people riding the Slingshot at the Texas State Fair. The Slingshot is a thrill ride that propels passengers about 90 meters (300 feet) into the air. Do an Internet search to find out more about this ride.

B. **Share your information.** Tell your partner what you found out.

C. **Discuss with a partner.** Would you like to ride the Slingshot? Why? What is the scariest ride you have ever been on?

CAPTION COMPETITION

What do you think the man is thinking? Tell a partner.

It is so hight, let me down.

▲ Two men ride the Slingshot at the Texas State Fair, U.S.A.

Review 1

A. Complete the sentences. Complete each sentence with one of the missing phrases.

> fight a lot   keep in touch with   have my back
> have a lot in common   hang out

1. I think you'll really like Peter when you meet him. You guys _have a lot in common_.
2. Thanks for helping me with my homework. You always _have my back_.
3. On the weekends, I like to _hang out_ with my friends at the mall.
4. My sister and I are not good friends. We always _fight a lot_.
5. I use Facebook to _keep in touch with_ my friends and acquaintances.

B. Do you agree or disagree with these statements? Discuss your answers with a partner. Make suggestions for something your partner can do to deal with his or her fear.

	Agree	Disagree
1. Giving presentations in English makes me nervous.	✓	
2. Flying freaks me out.		✓
3. Watching horror movies creeps me out.	✓	
4. I'm afraid of not getting good grades.	✓	
5. Earthquakes really scare me.	✓	

C. Look back at Units 1 and 2. What do the numbers refer to? Then find more numbers and ask your partner to guess what the numbers refer to.

1. 300–425 _most teens have their friends on Facebook._
2. 4-year-old _____.
3. 20% _afraid of mice_ _____.
   28%

D. Complete the questions with your own ideas. Then use your questions to interview your classmates.

1. How do you know _her._ (name)?
2. Do you use _Wechat_ (name of social network)?
3. Are you similar to _your mother_ (family member)?
4. Are you afraid of _fly_ (thing or situation)?
5. How can people deal with _stress_ (name of fear)?

Health

A man in a healing pool in
Karlovy Vary, Czech Republic

WARM UP

Answer these questions with a partner.

1. What things do you do to stay healthy? What things do you avoid?

2. There is a saying in English that "an apple a day keeps the doctor away." What do you think this means?

3. In the future, do you think most people will live longer or shorter lives?

Health myths or facts?

Healing touch being done on a patient
by a cardiologist and an assistant

LISTENING

A. Predict. Work with a partner. Guess: Are the statements below **true** or **false**?

	True or False?	Research shows . . .
1. Going outside with wet hair can make you sick.	F e	illnesses like a cold or the flu caused by a virus not going outside with wet head
2. Eating an apple a day keeps the doctor away.	F d,g	too many bad for teeth eat different type for
3. Eating food cooked in oil is bad for your skin.	F a	oil may prevent dangerous diseases like cancer including skin cancer
4. Looking at TV, computer, or cell phone screens for a long time is bad for your eyesight.	F b,f	good to look away from the screen every few minutes.

 B. Listen to check. Were your predictions in **A** correct?
Track 1-10

 C. Listen for details. What does the research show? Read the sentences below. Then listen
Track 1-10   and write the correct letters (**a–h**) in the table above. Two answers below are extra.

3 a. Some types may prevent cancer. 1 e. Viruses cause a cold or the flu.

4 b. You should look away often. 4 f. You can get a headache.

c. Too much of it can kill you. 2 g. It's high in vitamins and low in fat.

2 d. It's high in sugar. 1 h. It can make you feel cold.

D. Discuss with a partner. Look at the photo at the top of this page. Do you think you can
heal someone just by touching them? What does research show? Go online and find out.

CONVERSATION

Track 1-11 **A. Listen to the conversation.**

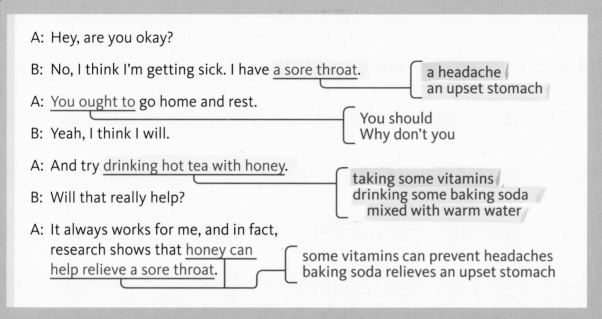

A: Hey, are you okay?

B: No, I think I'm getting sick. I have a sore throat.

> a headache
> an upset stomach

A: You ought to go home and rest.

> You should
> Why don't you

B: Yeah, I think I will.

A: And try drinking hot tea with honey.

> taking some vitamins
> drinking some baking soda
>   mixed with warm water

B: Will that really help?

A: It always works for me, and in fact, research shows that honey can help relieve a sore throat.

> some vitamins can prevent headaches
> baking soda relieves an upset stomach

B. Practice with a partner. Use the words on the right.

C. Practice again. Imagine that you're not feeling well. Explain what's wrong. **See page 115 for ideas.** Your partner will give you some advice.

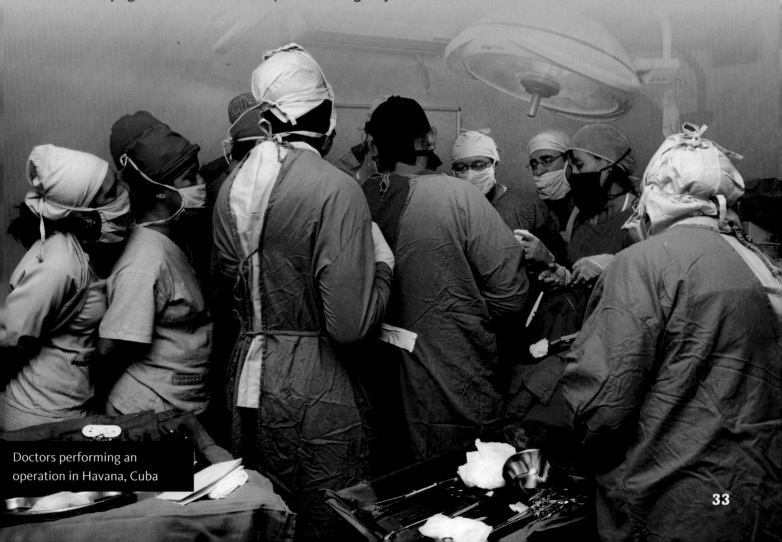

Doctors performing an operation in Havana, Cuba

READING

A. Discuss with a partner. Answer these questions. *My Grandfather*

1. Who is the oldest person you know? Why do you think that person has lived so long?

   He/She . . .   a. has good genes   b. has a healthy diet   c. other: _____

2. Read the title and the first paragraph of the reading below. In developed countries, how long are people living today? *75 years old* How long will people live in the future? *120 years or older.*

Track 1-12 **B. Split reading. Student A:** Now read the second paragraph and answer the questions in the chart below, under "Student A." **Student B: Turn to 114, and follow the directions there.**

	Student A	Student B
1. What are scientists studying?	*why exactly the bowhead whale and the rougheye rockfish live so long.*	
2. What have they learned?	*genes that control levels of sugar in the blood*	

LIVING TO
120+

These babies may live to be 120, thanks to new discoveries in science.

How long can humans live? In most developed countries, people are now living an average of 75 years. But scientists are trying to find ways to lengthen our lives—perhaps to 120 years or older—and to help us remain young as we age.

To do this, scientists are studying animals like the bowhead whale and the rougheye rockfish—both of which can live to over 200 years old—to learn why exactly these animals live so long. Recently, scientists studying worms and mice found genes that control the levels of sugar in the blood. When scientists "turn off" or reduce the activity of these genes, the animals live much longer. The mice, for example, lived up to 33% longer. The worms lived twice as long and still looked young and healthy when they died. There are similar genes in humans, and scientists are working to understand how they work so they can use them to help humans live longer.

C. Work in pairs. Ask your partner the questions in the chart on page 34. Write his or her answers under "Student B."

D. Discuss with a partner. Would you like to live to be 120 years old? Why or why not?

No. Too long and lonely

LISTENING

Track 1-14

A. Listen for opinions. Does each speaker think that living to 120 is a good idea? Listen and circle **yes** or **no**.

Speaker	Is living to 120 a good idea?	Why?
Man	(yes) / no	1. We'll have ~~more time~~ *write* to do things. 2. Scientists are working to _cure_ diseases and _slow_ aging. *(v)*
Woman	yes / (no)	1. Many older people have _health problems_. 2. It isn't _good for_ the planet.

Track 1-14

B. Listen for details. Write the man's and woman's reasons. Use one or two words.

Bolivian farmer Carmelo Flores ▶ was born in 1890, making him the world's oldest man.

DISCUSSION

Debating an issue and disagreeing politely. Work with a partner. What do you think about living to 120? Listen to your partner's opinion. Then disagree, using the language below. Make sure you give reasons to support your opinion.

> In my opinion / If you ask me, it's a great idea. For one thing . . .

> Really? I completely disagree. Many older people . . .

> I know what you mean / I know what you're saying, but scientists are working to . . .

NOW HEAR THIS

▲ An artificial ear growing around an ear-shaped scaffold

BEFORE YOU WATCH

About the video. Worldwide, there are millions of people who need a **transplant** to replace a damaged **organ**; it might be a new kidney, a heart, or another body part. At one hospital in the U.S., doctors are **experimenting** with a new way to help people who need a new ear, using human **cells**.

take a body part of another person.

body part

trying something new

A. Vocabulary matching. Read **About the video**. Then use a word in **bold** to complete the sentences below.

use microscope to see.

1. There are billions of ___cell___ in your body, but they are too small to see.

2. The heart is your body's hardest-working ___organ___. It beats 100,000 times a day—about 40 million times a year.

3. Doctors are ___experimenting___ with a new drug. They're testing it to see if it can cure the common cold.

   treat / fix / make it well

   cure your cool

4. A(n) ___transplant___ is a medical operation in which one person's body part is removed and another person's body part is put in.

B. Predict. Watch the video without the sound. Explain to your partner how the doctors make an artificial ear.

36

WHILE YOU WATCH

A. Watch the video. Check your answer in **Before You Watch B**. Then put the steps of the process below in order from **1–4**.

_4_ Attach the ear to a human. *connect*

_3_ Put the scaffold into the bioreactor to grow the ear. *85/190*

_1_ Create an ear scaffold.

_2_ Add living cells and food for the cells to the scaffold.

B. Watch again. Are the sentences below **true** or **false**?

	True	False
1. Doctors put the human ear onto the mouse to see if the ear keeps its shape.	✓	
2. Doctors chose to make an ear first because ears have few blood vessels.	✓	
3. Ears are easy to make because they have a simple shape.		✓
4. Doctors can make an artificial ear in only a few days.		✓

2 weeks to grow in bioreactor.

AFTER YOU WATCH

Talk with a partner. Use the expressions on page 35 to discuss your opinions.

1. Do you think it is OK to use animals like the mouse in the video for medical testing?
2. *same DNA / a copy* A clone is an exact copy of a plant or animal, made in a lab from the original plant's or animal's cells. Scientists are now experimenting with cloning, and in the future, cloning will allow us to bring back dead pets or extinct animals, create more animals and plants for food, and grow human cells to cure certain illnesses. We may even be able to clone humans. Do you think cloning is mostly a good or bad idea? Why?

◀ "CC" is the world's first cloned cat, produced at a university in Texas, U.S.A.

HEALTH DEBATE

You are going to have a debate about a health topic.

A. Work with a partner. Choose a health issue from the box. Then work on your own.
Student A: Think of two reasons to *support* this idea. **Student B:** Thinks of two reasons *against* the idea. Use at least one fact to support each reason.

- We should ban smoking (make it illegal) everywhere. *stop*
- Cosmetic surgery (to improve your appearance) is a good thing.
- People should become vegetarian.
- Unhealthy people should pay higher medical insurance.
- Your idea: _____

B. Debate the issue. Work with another pair. **Pair 1:** Tell the other pair your topic. Then have your debate. **Pair 2:** Listen to both sides. At the end, choose the winner of the debate. Then change roles.

> In my opinion, we ought to ban smoking everywhere. It's a very dangerous habit. Research by the World Health Organization says cigarettes kill almost six million people a year.

> I hear what you're saying, but . . .

C. Work in a group. Think about the two debates. What is your actual opinion on each topic? Explain and debate your ideas with your group.

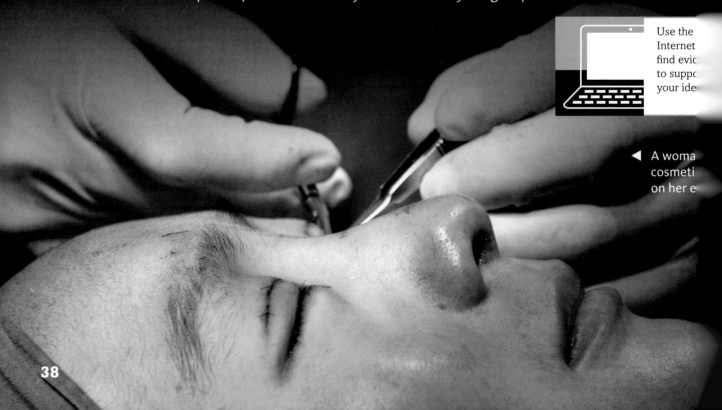

Use the
Internet
find evic
to suppo
your ide

◄ A woma
cosmeti
on her e

38

Change

A young boy watches TV in the early 1960s, and another plays a video game on a TV today.

WARM UP

Answer these questions with a partner.

1. When things change, do you usually feel nervous or excited?

2. Do you think life today is better than when your parents were young?

3. Can you name some recent big changes in your city or country?

39

MILLENNIALS
BORN BETWEEN 1982 AND 2000

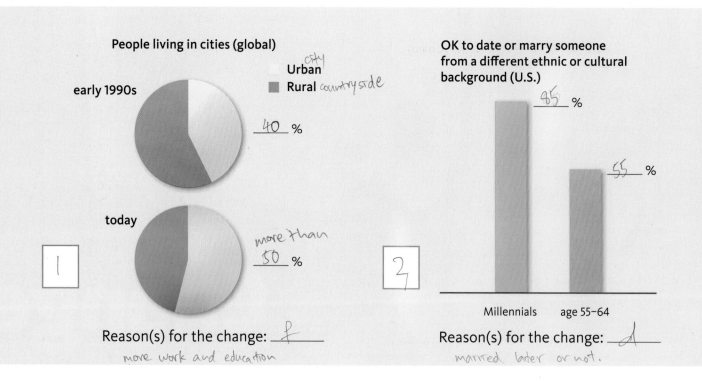

People living in cities (global)

☐ Urban *city*
■ Rural *countryside*

early 1990s

_40_ %

today

more than
_50_ %

[1]

Reason(s) for the change: _f_
more work and education

OK to date or marry someone from a different ethnic or cultural background (U.S.)

_85_ %

_55_ %

Millennials   age 55–64

[2]

Reason(s) for the change: _d_
married later or not.

LISTENING

A. Discuss with a partner. Answer these questions.
  1. When were people in the Millennial generation born? Are you a Millennial?   *1982 – 2000*   *Yes*
  2. Look at the four charts above. What do you think each chart shows?

🎧 Track 1-15 **B. Listen for gist.** You will hear a talk about people in the Millennial generation and how they compare to earlier generations. Number the charts (**1–4**) in the order they are talked about.

🎧 Track 1-15 **C. Listen for details.** Complete the labels on the charts with the correct number(s).

🎧 Track 1-15 **D. Listen for cause and effect.** What has caused the changes in charts **1–4**? Listen and write the reason(s) for change (**a–f**) on a chart. One chart has two answers, and one answer is extra.

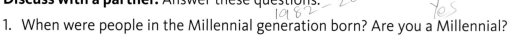

2 a. Families have more money.
2 b. People are having fewer children.
4 c. People want a good job first.

3 d. People have access to the Internet.
4 e. People are harder to please.
1 f. People are moving for work and school opportunities.

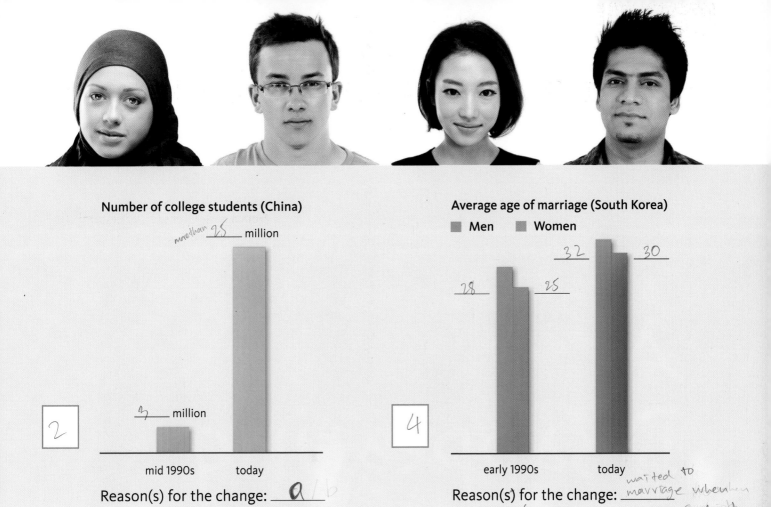

Number of college students (China)

more than ~~25~~ million

~~3~~ million

mid 1990s   today

 2

Reason(s) for the change: _a / b_
more money to spend

Average age of marriage (South Korea)

■ Men   ■ Women

28   32   25   30

early 1990s   today

4

Reason(s) for the change: _marriage when_ waited to
_e / c_ have a good job.

CONVERSATION

Track 1-16

A. Listen to the conversation.

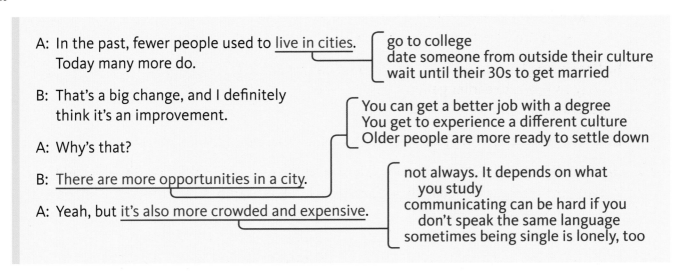

A: In the past, fewer people used to <u>live in cities</u>.
   Today many more do.

    go to college
    date someone from outside their culture
    wait until their 30s to get married

B: That's a big change, and I definitely
   think it's an improvement.

A: Why's that?

    You can get a better job with a degree
    You get to experience a different culture
    Older people are more ready to settle down

B: <u>There are more opportunities in a city</u>.

A: Yeah, but <u>it's also more crowded and expensive</u>.

    not always. It depends on what
      you study
    communicating can be hard if you
      don't speak the same language
    sometimes being single is lonely, too

B. Practice with a partner. Use the words on the right.

C. Practice again with your partner. Which changes in charts **1–4** are true for your
   country? Explain how things used to be and how they are today. Do you think the
   changes are positive or negative? Why?

A Disappearing Culture

▲ Kalash girls on their way to school

READING

A. Predict. Read only the title of the passage and look at the photos. Answer the questions.

1. Who is Sayed Gul Kalash?   2. What do you think is happening to the Kalash people?

Track 1-17

B. Split reading. Student A: Read the passage on this page. **Student B: Turn to page 116 and read the passage there.**

In Northern Pakistan, near the Afghan border, there is a group of people called the Kalasha. Once powerful and widespread, the Kalash civilization used to number tens of thousands of people; today, there are only about 3,500. In just a few generations, this culture—which is over 3,000 years old—may disappear.

Sayed Gul Kalash, a member of this community, is working to keep traditional elements of her culture alive, including its language. "Our language, spoken since 1,000 BCE, has no written script," she explains. But the culture's early history, stories, and songs have a lot to teach us about ourselves and the human experience, says Gul Kalash. She is trying to preserve the language by writing down these stories and songs for the first time.

C. **Work in pairs.** Ask your partner questions to help you answer the questions below.

1. How old is Kalash culture? How many Kalash people did there use to be? How many are there today?

2. Why could the Kalash language easily die out?

3. How is Sayed Gul Kalash trying to preserve Kalash culture?

4. The number of Kalash people is decreasing. What is causing this change?

D. **Discuss with your partner.** What are the pros and cons of moving away from a small culture like the Kalasha?

Sayed Gul Kalash works to preserve the Kalash culture and language.

LISTENING

Track 1-19

A. **Listen for details.** You will hear an interview about other things Sayed Gul Kalash is doing to preserve her culture. Listen and circle the correct answers in **1–3**.

Sayed Gul Kalash wants to . . .	If this happens . . .
1. train more Kalash (**teachers / historians**). ●	● a. people will want to protect Kalash culture.
	● b. children can go to school in their own village.
2. open a (**museum / store**). ●	● c. it might be bad for the environment.
3. (**stop / increase**) tourism. ●	● d. outsiders will learn about Kalash culture.
	● e. the Kalash will be able to build schools.
	● f. children will learn their language and culture.

Track 1-19

B. **Listen for consequences.** Match each answer in **1–3** with two consequences (**a–f**).

DISCUSSION

Talking about consequences. Work with a partner. Use your answers in **Listening B** to talk about Sayed Gul Kalash's ideas and the possible consequences. Use the language below to help you. Which of her ideas are the best? Share your answers with another pair.

> **If the Kalash train** more local teachers, **children will learn** their language and culture.

> Yeah, but **if they** only **learn** their own language, **they may not get** good jobs in the future.

JEJU ISLAND DIVERS

A haenyo from Jeju Island showing octopuses she has caught

BEFORE YOU WATCH

About the video. Haenyos are female divers who live on Jeju Island in Korea. They make money and support their families by diving for seafood. In the past, there used to be many haenyos on the island, but today, very few younger women are doing this work.

Predict. Why do you think fewer young women are becoming haenyos today?

WHILE YOU WATCH

A. Watch the video. Are the sentences below **true** or **false**? Correct the false sentences.

	True	False
1. In the past, most women wanted to become haenyos.		✓
2. Some haenyos are men.		✓
3. Being a haenyo is difficult, dangerous work.	✓	
4. Haenyos often spend five or more hours diving for seafood. *6 hours.*	✓	
5. Today's haenyos are all older than 50.		✓

45 - 75

B. Watch again. Answer the questions about Sunny Hong and her aunt.

1. What does Sunny Hong do for a living?

   Haenyos tour guide. / She is a tour guide.

2. How old is her aunt and when did she start diving?

   63   613 / She is 63. She started diving at age 13.

3. Does Sunny Hong want to be a haenyo?

   No. She wants a job that lets her use her English skills.

AFTER YOU WATCH

Work with a partner. Discuss the questions. Then share your answers with another pair.

1. What's causing the change on Jeju Island? _touri_
2. What do you think the consequences will be if the haenyos disappear? _result / what happen_
3. Do you think Jeju Island should try to preserve the haenyo tradition? Why? _protect_

   Young Jeju women have access to better education now, and

▼ Haenyo divers collecting shellfish

CHANGING TIMES

You are going to give a timed talk on a change that is happening in your city or country.

A. Work with a partner. Choose an idea from the box below or think of your own. Answer questions **1–5**. Then prepare a three-minute talk.

- something related to work, school, shopping, family, or gender roles
- a neighborhood or area of your city
- a pop-culture or fashion trend

1. What's changing?
2. How were things in the past? How are they now?
3. What's causing the change?
4. What will the consequences of this change be?
5. Do you think this change is positive or negative?

B. Work in a small group. Take turns giving your timed talk to the group. The others listen and take notes. Each person should explain if they agree or disagree with the speaker.

Look online for photos and videos as well as facts and statistics to use in your presentation.

C. Work in a new group. Repeat your talk with a new group.

A lot of small neighborhood stores are disappearing. In the past, a lot of people used to shop in these places, but today, more people go to supermarkets and department stores or they buy stuff online.

▼ Women ride Segway scooters in New Delhi, India

THINK ABOUT THE PHOTO

Examine the photo. Look at the photo on the next page. Check (✓) all of the things below that you can find. Add a few words of your own to the list.

☐ elderly woman ☐ walking stick ☐ robotic leg ☐ therapist ☐ stairs

☐ wheelchair _____ _____ _____

DISCUSSION

A. **Learn more online.** This photo shows an 89-year-old woman using Hybrid Assistive Limb (HAL) robotic legs to help her get around. Therapists from the Akanekai Showa Hospital, Japan, are helping her. Do an Internet search to find out more about HAL.

B. **Share your information.** Tell your partner what you found out about HAL.

C. **Describe the photo.** Work in pairs. Take turns describing the photo to each other.

> There are two therapists in the picture. The therapists are helping the woman to walk across the room.

D. **Look at the photo again.** Imagine you can interview the therapists in the picture. What questions will you ask? Make a list.

E. **Interview your partner.** Take turns as interviewer and therapist.

CAPTION COMPETITION

What do you think the woman is saying? Tell a partner.

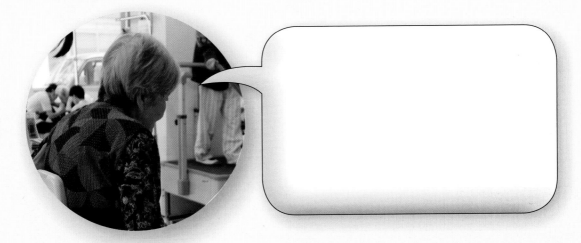

◄ An 89-year-old woman using Hybrid Assistive Limb robotic legs at the Akanekai Showa Hospital, Japan

Review 2

A. Unscramble the illnesses from Unit 3. Then add one of your own and ask your partner to unscramble it.

1. ahcadeeh   _____

2. hoguc   _____

3. eht ufl   _____

4. reevf   _____

5. your idea: _____

B. Complete the sentences. Match **1–5** with **a–e** to make sentences.

1. If more people live in the city,   ●   ● a. they might have fewer children.

2. If fewer young women become haenyos,   ●   ● b. it is easier to remember them.

3. If couples marry later,   ●   ● c. it will become more crowded.

4. If we write things down,   ●   ● d. the tradition may disappear.

5. If there is no tourism in the area,   ●   ● e. it is difficult for local people to make money.

C. Complete each sentence. Use vocabulary from Unit 3 or Unit 4.

1. If you are getting _____, you are starting to feel unwell. For example, you may have a sore throat.

2. If you are a _____, you study things about the natural world.

3. If you need a new heart, you go to hospital for a(n) _____

   _____.

4. If you are a _____, you were born between 1982 and the year 2000.

5. If you try to _____ a culture, you try to stop it from disappearing.

D. Debate an issue with a partner. One person should agree and the other person should disagree.

Issue: *It is better to live in the city than the country.*

Success

Explorer Richard E. Byrd is shown here at the
research station he built in Antarctica. He led
four successful expeditions to the South Pole.

sped

good on the big trip.
like climbing a mountain.

Leve 4 s/L.

WARM UP

Answer these questions with a partner.

1. Look at the photo. What difficulties
   do you think Byrd had to overcome
   to achieve success?
2. Name a successful person. Why
   is the person successful?
3. The opposite of success is failure.
   Is failure always a bad thing?

51

The Key to Success

"When people tell me things are impossible, it just gives me energy," says Saudi scientist and business-woman Hayat Sindi.

LISTENING

A. Rank and discuss. To be successful in life, how important do you think these things are? Choose your top three, and rank them from **1–3**. Compare answers with a partner.

◯ a good education	◯ determination	◯ intelligence
◯ clear goals	◯ good looks	◯ luck
◯ connections	◯ hard work	◯ self-confidence

B. Listen and check. Listen and circle the two answers in **A** to complete the sentence below.

Track 1-20

To be successful in life, _____ and _____ are the two most important factors, says psychologist Angela Lee Ducksworth.

C. Listen for details. Look at the photo and read about scientist Hayat Sindi. Then listen. Circle the correct answers below.

Track 1-21

1. Hayat Sindi went to England _____.

   a. to go to university   b. for a job   c. to help her family

2. Which sentence about her time in England is NOT true?

   a. At first, she couldn't speak English.
   b. Once, she was so lonely she returned home.
   c. She was the first Saudi woman in her biotechnology program.

3. Hayat Sindi's company _____.

   a. helps sick people in poor countries
   b. trains doctors around the world
   c. organizes science contests

4. To make money for her company, Hayat Sindi _____.

   a. taught science   b. entered two contests   c. had to borrow money

D. Discuss with a partner. Answer these questions.

1. Look again at the two most important factors for success in **B**. How does Hayat Sindi's experience show this?

2. What about you? When something is difficult, do you usually keep trying or give up? Give an example from your life.

▼ The paper medical test created by Sindi's company that instantly tests people for disease

CONVERSATION

A. Listen to the conversation.

Track 1-22

A: One of my goals is to <u>get a part-time job this summer</u>.

    visit France after graduation
    improve my English this term
    start my own business someday

B: Sounds good. What's your plan?

A: Well, first I'm going to <u>visit the school's online career center</u>.

    learn to speak French
    participate more in class
    make a website

B: Good idea.

A: Then I'm going to <u>create a résumé and send it out</u>.

    save money for the trip
    read more in English
    get work experience

B: Good luck. I hope it works out!

B. Practice with a partner. Use the words on the right.

C. Practice again. Talk about your own goals.

READING

A. Work with a partner. Answer the questions below.

1. Have you ever _____? How did you feel?

> . . . failed a school exam   . . . been turned down (rejected) when asking someone on a date
>
> . . . lost a sports game   . . . failed a driving test

2. Read the title of the passage. What is your answer?

B. Read the article. As you read, think about your answer to the question in the title.

Track 1-23

C. Reading comprehension. Work with a partner. Answer these questions.

1. What can failure teach us? In your own words, explain one of the lessons from the passage.
2. What advice is given in the last paragraph? Do you agree with it?

FAILURE:
WHAT CAN WE LEARN FROM IT?

The crew of ▲ Apollo 13. Their mission to the moon failed when their rocket had problems. But all of the astronauts returned safely to Earth.

In life, there's a lot of pressure to be successful in school, on the playing field, at work, and in our personal relationships. And yet, at some point, we will all lose a game, fail an exam, or be turned down for a job or a date. Failure is hard to deal with, but there are some important lessons it can teach us.

LESSON 1: Learn from your mistakes. Think about what you did wrong and how you can do things differently in the future. "I learned how *not* to climb Mount Everest the first four times I tried," says mountain climber Pete Athans. After studying his mistakes and making changes to his plan, Athans finally reached the top of Everest on the fifth try.

LESSON 2: Be careful. Very often, when everything's going right, it can be easy to be careless and make mistakes. Maybe you did poorly on a test because you thought you knew everything and didn't study enough. Failures like this remind us that things can go wrong and that we need to be careful.

No one likes failure, but it's important not to give up. Failure is an opportunity to learn and grow. "There's no magic to getting where we already know we can get," says Athans. Successful people keep trying, even when they fail.

LISTENING

A. Predict. Look at the photo and read the caption. Why do you think the Apple Newton failed? Make some guesses.

🎧 Track 1-24 **B. Listen for details.** You will hear a lecture. Write a word or two in each blank below.

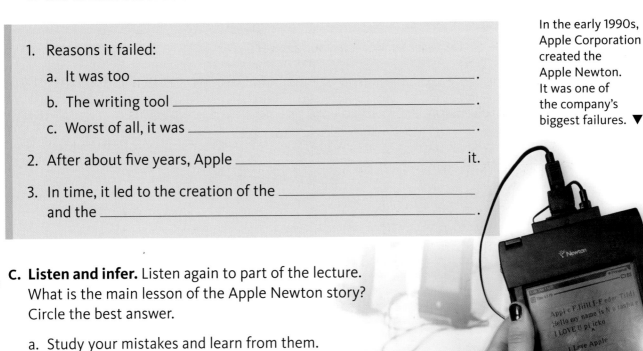

In the early 1990s, Apple Corporation created the Apple Newton. It was one of the company's biggest failures. ▼

1. Reasons it failed:

    a. It was too _____ .

    b. The writing tool _____ .

    c. Worst of all, it was _____ .

2. After about five years, Apple _____ it.

3. In time, it led to the creation of the _____ and the _____ .

🎧 Track 1-25 **C. Listen and infer.** Listen again to part of the lecture. What is the main lesson of the Apple Newton story? Circle the best answer.

a. Study your mistakes and learn from them.

b. Only try if you are experienced.

c. If you're careful, you won't fail.

d. Bad things happen for no reason sometimes.

DISCUSSION

Explaining a result. Talk about a time you (or someone you know) didn't succeed at first. What happened? What did you (or the person) learn from the experience? Use the language below to explain.

My friend asked a girl on a date and she turned him down.

What did he do?

He thought about it and knew she liked music, so he wrote her a love song.

Did it work?

Yes! Eventually / In time / In the end she became his girlfriend.

ANTARCTIC CHALLENGE

BEFORE YOU WATCH

About the video. Jon Krakauer is an adventure writer who understands failure. He almost died in a severe snowstorm on Mount Everest that killed 12 other climbers, including members of his own team. After this, Jon wasn't sure he wanted to continue climbing. Now, he's in Antarctica to be part of the first team to climb Rakekniven Peak.

Discussion. Look at the photo and read **About the video.** Then answer the questions.

1. What failure did Krakauer experience?
2. Why is Krakauer in Antarctica? What are his goals?

Queen Maud Land, Antarctica

▲ Rakekniven Peak is part of a mountain range in Antarctica. At about 610 meters high, the peak is very steep and difficult to climb.

WHILE YOU WATCH

A. Watch the video. As you watch, put the events of the team's journey in order from **1** to **7**.

_____ The team travels over 60 km to Rakekniven Peak.

_____ After a ten-day climb, the team reaches the top.

_____ The weather improves and the team starts the climb again.

_____ Krakauer places a flag on the peak.

_____ The team begins their climb.

_____ The team sleeps on the mountain.

_____ There's a storm and the team has to go back down.

B. Vocabulary matching. You heard these sentences in the video. What do the words in **blue** mean? Circle **a** or **b**.

1. Jon says, "If we get up this thing (Rakekniven), it will be a much more satisfying **accomplishment** than having climbed Everest."

    a. success   b. disappointment

2. "The final part of the climb is difficult . . . Despite the many **hardships**, Jon is determined to keep climbing."

    a. memories   b. challenges

AFTER YOU WATCH

Work in a small group. Discuss these questions.

1. How do you think Krakauer feels about climbing now? Do you think his success in climbing Rakekniven will help him forget his failure on Mount Everest?

2. What goals have you accomplished? How did you achieve your goals? Did you face any hardships to achieve them?

Jon Krakauer ▶
in his tent in
Antarctica

A Lifetime Achievement Award

You are going to nominate someone for a lifetime achievement award.

A. Work in pairs. With a partner, choose a person you think should get a lifetime achievement award. Answer the questions below. Using your answers, create a two- or three-minute presentation about the person. **See page 118 for help giving your presentation.**

1. Who is the person? Why should he or she get the award? Did he or she have to overcome any hardships or failures?
2. How has the person helped others? Give examples.
3. What can we learn from this person?
4. What important personal qualities does the person have? Use at least two words to describe the person during your presentation.

B. Work with two other pairs. Give your presentation. When you listen, take notes and answer the questions in **A** about each person. At the end, vote as a group for the best choice. The pair who gave this presentation moves on to the final.

C. Work as a class. Listen as the finalists from each group give their presentations. At the end, vote as a class for who should get the lifetime achievement award.

Find stories or quotes online about the person you choose.

◄ Actor Jackie Chan receives a lifetime achievement award for his work in movies.

6

Consumerism

Shoppers at the Suria KLCC Mall, in Kuala Lumpur, Malaysia

Warm Up

Answer these questions with a partner.

1. What was the last thing you bought? Where was it made?
2. Do you think *consumerism* is mostly good or bad?
3. What kind of consumer are you? Turn to page 120 and take the survey there.

Your Spending Habits

Consumer goods—such as cars and electronics—have made people's lives more comfortable, and increased demand for these things has created jobs. Unfortunately, however, buying more also has a negative impact on the environment.

LISTENING

A. Predict. Look at the photo above and read the caption. How might buying things like electronics, cars, or meat have a negative impact on the environment? Discuss with a partner.

Track **2-01**

B. Check your predictions. Listen and complete each problem in the chart below with one or two words or a number.

1. **PROBLEM** People _____ old items. Only _____% are recycled; the rest go in the _____.

   SOLUTION _____ and _____ older appliances, or safely _____ them.

2. **PROBLEM** There are almost _____ cars on the road worldwide. They use _____% of the world's oil and create _____% of the world's air pollution.

   SOLUTION Cities need to make it easy to _____, _____, or use public transportation.

3. **PROBLEM** Producing less than _____ grams of beef requires _____ liters of water, which is wasteful. Large numbers of animals also live in small spaces, which can lead to the spread of _____.

   SOLUTION People need to _____ less _____.

60

Track 2-01

C. Listen for details. What solutions does the speaker suggest? Complete each solution in the chart with one or two words.

D. Discuss with a partner. Look at your answers in the chart. How can we reduce the negative impact our shopping choices have on the environment?

CONVERSATION

Track 2-02

A. Listen to the conversation.

A: Would you rather <u>own a bike or a car</u>?   [live in a big or small house
                                                    repair or replace a broken cell phone

B: <u>A bike</u>, definitely. It's <u>less expensive</u>. How about you?

A: I'd rather <u>own a small car</u>.   [own a big house / replace it   [A small house / easier to care for

B: Really?   Repair it / better for the environment

A: Yeah. It's a lot <u>more comfortable</u>.   [more spacious / less hassle

B. Practice with a partner. Use the words on the right.

C. Practice again. Give your own opinions. In general, are your purchasing preferences mostly good or bad for the environment?

▼ A computer hard drive resting on a pile of shredded hard drives

READING

A. Predict. Which countries do you think are a major source of the products in the box? Match each product (**a–d**) to the places you think are its major sources (**1–4**).

> a. bananas   b. coffee   c. cotton   d. electronics

1. _____ Vietnam   2. _____ Pakistan   3. _____ the Philippines   4. _____ South Korea

Track 2-03

B. Read the passage. Check and correct your ideas in **A.**

Where does **your stuff** come from?

In today's global marketplace, many of the products we buy are made or grown somewhere else.

Most of the coffee you drink, for example, is probably imported from Brazil or Vietnam—two of the world's largest coffee producers. Many of the everyday foods we eat are also imported. Most of the world's cacao (the bean used to make chocolate) is grown in two African nations: the Ivory Coast and Ghana. And a lot of the fruit we enjoy all year round comes from somewhere else. For example, 75% of the world's bananas—the world's most popular exported fruit—are grown in just four countries: Ecuador, Costa Rica, Colombia, and the Philippines.

The clothing industry has been global for decades. Most of the world's cotton, which is used to make clothes, is grown in China, India, the U.S., and Pakistan. A lot of it is then shipped to developing nations in Asia and Latin America, where many pants, shirts, and other clothes are made.

You can check any of these statistics on your phone or laptop, both of which were probably designed in North America, South Korea, or Europe, and then made somewhere in Asia, most likely China. Though China is now the world's largest electronics manufacturer, a lot of the natural resources that are used to make devices like phones and computers come from African countries like the Democratic Republic of Congo, which are rich in resources such as diamonds, gold, and tin.

C. Discussion. How many of the items in **A** did you guess correctly? Did any of this information surprise you?

▼ Most clothing sold in developed countries is made overseas in factories like this one in Cambodia.

LISTENING

Track 2-04 **A. Listen for gist.** You will hear a speaker talk about the global marketplace. Which of the issues below does the speaker talk about?

☐ bad working conditions and low pay   ☐ environmental problems

☐ children working   ☐ bad treatment of animals

Track 2-04 **B. Listen for details.** Complete the notes below with one or two words or numbers.

1. Some factory workers work _____ a day, and factory _____ have killed people. Many earn less than _____ a day.

2. In the Democratic Republic of Congo, _____% of gold miners are children.

3. In the Amazon, many trees have been cut down to grow _____ and raise _____.

4. To produce half a kilogram of diamonds, miners remove _____ kilograms of earth.

C. Discuss with a partner. Look at the three issues you checked in **A**. What can we do about these issues?

DISCUSSION

Using the passive voice. Work in a small group. Answer these questions using the language below.

1. Think of something you ate today. Where was it grown? Was it imported?

2. Look at two items of clothing you're wearing right now. Where were they made?

3. Think of all the items your group talked about. Were most grown or made in your country, or were they imported? Do you think people or the environment were hurt to make these things?

> I drank a coffee this morning. The beans were imported from Guatemala.

> I bought these boots in London, but they were made in Turkey.

Diamond mining results in large holes in the Earth. This mine in Russia goes down over 600 meters (2,000 feet). ▶

The Carbon Footprint of a Cheeseburger

the cheese

the burger

the bun

Between 3.6 and 6.1 kilograms of greenhouse gases are produced to make just one cheeseburger.

BEFORE YOU WATCH

About the video. Jamais Cascio studies global warming. In this video, he looks at the carbon footprint of a cheeseburger, and examines how the process of making cheeseburgers produces greenhouse gases like carbon dioxide (CO_2) and methane (CH_4) from burning fossil fuels and raising cows.

A. Vocabulary matching. Read **About the video**. Then use the words in blue to complete the sentences below.

_____ is an increase in the Earth's temperature. One factor that causes it is our use of _____ (oil, gas, and coal). When we burn these fuels, they release _____ like carbon dioxide into the air. In large amounts, these gases trap heat and cause Earth to get warmer. This can lead to extreme weather and other dangerous environmental changes. The solution to this problem is for each person to reduce his or her _____.

B. Predict. What steps are involved in making a cheeseburger? How can these affect global warming? Share your ideas with a partner.

A. Watch the video. Complete the labels in the diagram with one or two words.

Cows produce a lot of _____, including methane.

Food for cows requires a lot of _____.

Meat has to be kept _____.

Wheat for buns requires a lot of _____.

You have to _____ meat from place to place.

B. Watch again. Match **1–4** with a word or number (**a–g**). Three answers are extra.

1. The number of people in the United States: _____
2. The number of cheeseburgers each American eats in a week on average: _____
3. The amount of metric tons of CO_2 that is produced each year from eating cheeseburgers: _____
4. That's more CO_2 than all the _____ in the U.S. produce.

a. cows
b. 200 million
c. 150 billion
d. 2
e. 300 million
f. SUVs (large cars)
g. 3

AFTER YOU WATCH

A. Talk with a partner. At the end of the video, the speaker says, "Scientists are trying to find ways to stop global warming, but you and I might be able to do something about it right now." What can we do?

B. Survey your classmates. With your partner, add three more questions to the shopping survey below. Then interview your classmates. Summarize your findings for another pair.

To protect the environment, would you be willing to . . .	Yes, definitely.	No, I'd rather not.
1. buy no meat / become a vegetarian?		
2. only buy goods made in your country?		

RESEARCH AN EVERYDAY ITEM

You are going to research where an everyday item comes from.

A. Work with a partner. Choose an item from one of the categories below. Research this product by answering questions **1–4**. Using your answers, create a 2–3 minute presentation. You can create a poster or use photos and video.

- a kind of drink
- a food
- an article of clothing or an accessory
- an electronic device
- a piece of jewelry
- your idea: _____

1. Where is the product made or grown? Who makes it?

2. What is the product (and its packaging) made of—plastic, glass, a metal of some kind, cotton, leather, something else? Where does this material come from?

3. Once the product is made, where is it sold and for how much?

4. On a scale from 1 (*not at all*) to 5 (*yes, definitely*), how good do you think the product is for people? How environmentally friendly do you think it is? Are there similar products that would be better to buy?

B. Join three other pairs. Pair 1: Give your presentation. **Pairs 2, 3, and 4:** Listen and take notes by answering questions **1–4** in **A**. Take turns to present.

C. Work as a class. Are there any products you will or won't buy in the future? Which was the best product you learned about? Why?

Look online for more information about your item and videos or photos of how it is made.

These tea pickers in India are part of a group that provides "fair trade tea." This means that the pickers have good working conditions and get good pay for their work.

The Big Picture 3

THINK ABOUT THE PHOTO

A. Examine the photo. Look at the photo on the next page. Check (✓) all of the things below that you can find. Add a few words of your own to the list.

☐ trophy   ☐ suit   ☐ bow tie   ☐ necklace   ☐ spots

☐ lapels   _____ _____ _____

B. Learn about the photo. Complete the description of the photo by choosing the correct words.

In this photo, Lionel Messi of **1.** (**Argentina** / **Brazil**) is receiving the 2012 FIFA Player of the Year **2.** (**award** / **certificate**). Messi **3.** (**broke** / **won**) the world record with 91 goals scored in a year. Abby Wambach of the United States is receiving her FIFA Women's Player of the Year trophy. Wambach scored five goals in London as the U.S. **4.** (**won** / **lost**) its third straight gold medal at the **5.** (**Olympics** / **World Cup**).

DISCUSSION

A. Learn more online. Do an Internet search about Lionel Messi and Amy Wambach.

B. Share your information. Tell your partner what you found out.

C. Think about the photo. Would you like to be famous? Why or why not?

D. Interview your classmates. Have you ever received an award or trophy? If so, what for?

CAPTION COMPETITION

What do you think Lionel Messi is thinking? Tell a partner.

◀ Lionel Messi and
Abby Wambach

A. Vocabulary review. Complete each sentence using the words in the box.

> turned   failed   produced   determined   replaced

1. John is very _____ to do well in his exams.

2. I'm sad because I _____ my driver's license test.

3. Susan asked George on a date, but he _____ her down.

4. My car broke down yesterday. The battery had to be _____.

5. 66% of greenhouse gases are _____ by the things humans do.

B. What do you remember? Look back at Unit 5. Are the following statements **true** or **false**?

	True	False
1. Richard E. Byrd led successful expeditions to the Arctic.	____	____
2. Hayat Sindi's family was happy for her to go to England.	____	____
3. The Apple Newton was very light.	____	____
4. The Apple Newton helped Apple develop better products.	____	____
5. Jon Krakauer has climbed to the top of Mount Everest.	____	____

C. Make a quiz. Look back at Unit 6 and write some statements that are true and some that are false. Ask your partner to say whether they are true or false.

D. One-minute presentations. Work with a partner. Use a stopwatch and talk about each of the following topics for one minute. Your partner will time you and tell you when to switch topics. Then swap.

- *one of your goals for the future*
- *a time you didn't succeed*
- *ways you can help protect the environment*
- *products that are made or grown in your country*

7

Art

A young girl walks along a painted fence in the Republic of the Seychelles.

WARM UP

Answer these questions with a partner.

1. Are you interested in art? What kinds of art do you like?

2. Look at the photo. Is this a work of art? Why or why not? Is street art common in your city?

3. How is street art different from the art you see in galleries or museums?

MODERN ART

A sculpture at Beijing 798 Art
District, China (artist unknown)

Dots Obsession by Yayoi Kusuma

LISTENING

A. Work with a partner. Look at the descriptive language on page 121. Then use some of the
words to describe the art you see on this page.

Track 2-05 **B. Listen for gist.** Number each piece of art (**1–4**) in the order the people talk about them.

Track 2-05 **C. Listen for opinions.** How do the man and woman feel about each piece? Listen and choose
likes or **doesn't like**.

	the man		the woman	
	likes	doesn't like	likes	doesn't like
1.				
2.				
3.				
4.				

Track 2-05 **D. Listen for details.** For each piece of art, circle the statement that is NOT true.

1. a. The style was very common at the time.
    b. It is an example of abstract art.
    c. The artist's work sells for a lot of money.

2. a. It was done by a well-known artist.
    b. It was first shown in China.
    c. They are all different.

3. a. It is an example of pop art.
    b. It uses a favorite symbol of the artist.
    c. It was done by a man.

4. a. The name of the piece means "child."
    b. It was inspired by the artist's parent.
    c. It is nearly nine meters tall.

CONVERSATION

Track 2-06
A. Listen to the conversation.

A: Check out this <u>painting</u>.

                                             display of sculpted heads
                                             dot installation
                                             giant spider sculpture

B: Hmmm. It's <u>really interesting</u>.

                                             very cool
                                             kind of fun
                                             absolutely incredible

A: I don't know. I think it's <u>kind of silly</u>.

B: Really?

                                             just okay
                                             sort of weird

A: Yeah, <u>I'm over</u> this kind of art.

                                             a bit scary
                          I'm not really into
                          I just don't get

B: Not me. I love it.

                          I'm kind of freaked out by

B. Practice with a partner. Use the words on the right.

C. Practice again. Talk about the art in this lesson. What do you think of it? Why? Then search for other pieces of art online and talk about them.

One Number 31 by Jackson Pollock

Maman by Louise Bourgeois

73

READING

Track 2-07

A. Predict. Look at the photos and the title of the reading. What does this street artist do? Read to check your ideas.

STREET ARTIST JR: THE PRINCE OF PRINTS

If you live in a city, you've probably seen the work of street artists. Whether you think it's ugly or beautiful, it often inspires you to see a place or think about an idea in a new way.

For the past 13 years, French street artist JR—who won't reveal his full name—has been putting photographs on outdoor surfaces throughout the world, often risking arrest because his photos seem to take on political meaning. As part of his current project, which he calls *Inside Out*, JR invites people to take self-portraits. He enlarges the images and returns them to people, who then place them on buildings, public transportation, and other places. Along with each photo is a message explaining what is most important to the person. The goal, says JR, is to show others in the community—and the world—who you are and what you care about most.

Over 100,000 self-portraits have appeared in countries all over the world; there's even one at the North Pole. Viewers are fascinated by the enlarged images, and even those who don't approve of street art agree that it's hard to look away from the portraits—faces filled with laughter, anger, wonder, or sorrow. "The beauty is that these photos can appear anywhere," says JR. "I love when this happens—when art appears in places that you would not necessarily expect it to. And the best part is that anyone can [see] it. Why shouldn't everyone enjoy it?"

B. Reading comprehension. Answer the questions in your own words with a partner.

1. Explain how JR's *Inside Out* project works.
2. What is the purpose of this project?
3. Has the project been popular? What do people think of it?
4. How does JR feel about this kind of street art?

▼ Photos from J.R.'s *Inside Out* show in Times Square, New York

C. Discuss with a partner. Do an online search for JR's *Inside Out* project and look at some of the self-portraits there. What do you think of them? Would you like to participate in this project? What would your message be?

▲ Faces on a wall in Paris, from JR's earlier piece, *Face 2 Face*

LISTENING

Track 2-08

A. Listen for opinions. Listen and circle the correct answers.

1. How do the speakers feel about JR's work?
   a. They both like it.   b. The woman likes it.   c. The man likes it.

2. How do they feel about graffiti in general?
   a. They both like it.   b. The woman likes it.   c. The man likes it.

Track 2-08

B. Listen for details. Look at your answers above. Then read the sentences below. Can you remember any of the answers? Listen again and complete each word.

The woman's opinion about graffiti	The man's opinion about graffiti
1. Some graffiti is _a_____.	1. Most of it is _v_____.
2. Some of the artists have real _t_____.	2. It's _u_____.
3. Their work makes a public space more _i_____.	3. Only the _g_____ stuff gets media attention.
4. It's great that it's _f_____.	4. The artists are doing it without _p_____.

DISCUSSION

Introducing another point of view. Work with a partner. Ask your partner what he or she thinks about graffiti. Then reply with another point of view (even if it's not really your own). Use the language below. Take turns.

> What do you think of graffiti?

> Some of it is kind of cool.

> I know what you mean, but a lot of it is also ugly, and it's expensive to clean up.

> Yeah, I guess, though … / I hear you, but … / Even so …

75

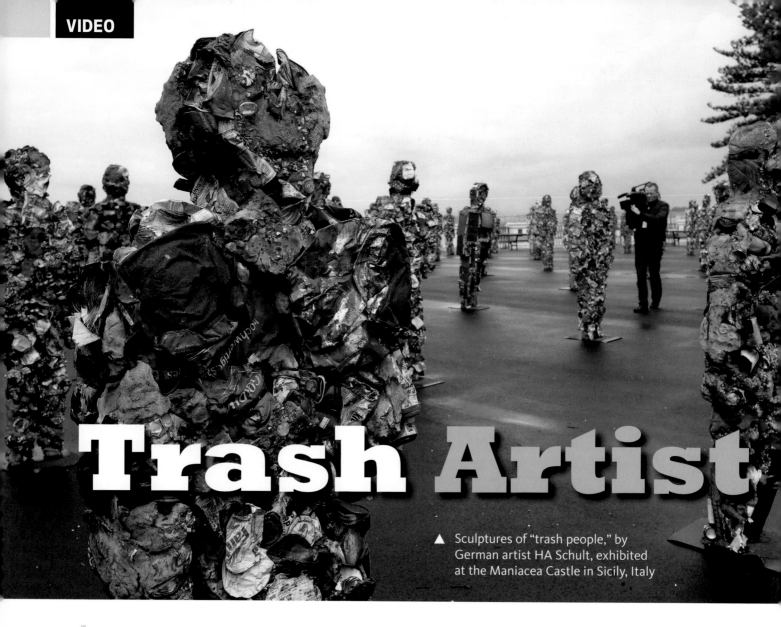

Trash Artist

▲ Sculptures of "trash people," by German artist HA Schult, exhibited at the Maniacea Castle in Sicily, Italy

BEFORE YOU WATCH

About the video. HA Schult is a German artist. He creates sculptures shaped like people from trash. He's taken this exhibit to cities all over the world. Even though these sculptures can't talk, there's a lot they have to tell us about garbage—and ourselves.

A. Work with a partner. Discuss the questions.

1. What kinds of things do you throw away (put in the garbage) every day?
2. Do you think you create a lot of garbage?
3. When you throw your trash away, do you know where it goes?

B. Predict. In the video, HA Schult says, "We are on the garbage planet." What do you think he means? What point do you think he is trying to make with his sculptures?

a. Garbage can be beautiful.

c. Each country's trash is unique.

b. Trash is a global problem.

d. A lot of art is garbage.

WHILE YOU WATCH

A. Watch the video. Check your answer in **Before You Watch B**.

B. Watch again. Read the information below. Then watch and complete the sentences.

1. Schult made his sculptures from trash he found in (**Germany** / **China**).

2. Schult says, "We know that the garbage of (**China** / **Korea**) comes to Europe. The garbage of Europe goes to (**Russia** / **England**) and that garbage goes to (**South Africa** / **South America**)."

3. Schult's first trash people exhibit was in Xanten, (**Germany** / **China**). Later the trash people appeared at (**the Kremlin** / **Red Square**) in Moscow, near (**the Great Wall** / **Tiananmen Square**) in China, near the Matterhorn mountain in Switzerland, and then near (**the Pyramids** / **Victoria Falls**) in Africa. Now, fifty sculptures are at National Geographic in (**Washington, D.C.** / **New York City**).

AFTER YOU WATCH

Talk with a partner. Discuss these questions.

1. Why do you think Schult chose the places above to show his sculptures?

2. Do you think his art will get people to think more about trash and the things they throw away?

▼ German artist HA Schult stands with his "trash people" below the pyramids in Giza, Egypt.

An Art Exhibition

You are going to organize and attend a class art exhibition.

A. Find a piece of art. Choose a piece of art that you like. Print a copy of it, or have it ready on screen.

B. Describe the art. Working alone, write this information about the artwork.
- The name of the piece (if there is one)
- The name of the artist
- The date or time period that the piece was created
- What you like most about the piece

C. Hold an art exhibition. Divide the class in half. **Group 1:** Arrange your artwork with its notes in the classroom. Stay with your artwork and be prepared to talk about it. **Group 2:** Look at all the artwork on display. Ask questions and take notes. As you walk around, tell others what you think of each piece. When you've finished, change roles.

D. Work with a partner. What were your three favorite pieces? Why? Did you learn anything new?

Research your artist online. Find out where the artist is from and look at other work he or she has done.

> I loved the Dali painting "The Persistence of Memory." His work was so original and interesting.

> Yeah, I know what you mean. I like that one, but it wasn't one of my favorites.

◀ A woman looks at Impressionist paintings in Baltimore, U.S.A.

8

Collaboration

People build a wall of sandbags
during a flood in California, U.S.A.

WARM UP

Answer these questions with a partner.

1. Do you prefer to collaborate with others or work on your own?

2. Give examples of times when you think it is better to work with others.

3. Have you ever donated money or volunteered your time to help others? What did you do?

Collective Intelligence

▲ Students at a school in
Nepal share a computer.

Foldit, an online ▶
science game

LISTENING

A. Discuss with a partner. Answer the questions.

1. What do you think the expression "two heads are better than one" means?

2. Do you know any websites where ordinary people can contribute their knowledge?

Track 2-09

B. Listen for gist. Listen to a speaker talking about online collaboration. What is NOT true about the websites Wikipedia and Foldit?

    a. They're useful collaborative tools.

    b. They're used worldwide.

    c. Most contributors to the sites are scientists.

    d. They rely on people adding information to them.

Track 2-09

C. Listen for details. Are the statements below **true** or **false**? Correct the false statements.

	True	False
1. Wikipedia has millions of articles in about 20 languages.	___	___
2. Scientists doing AIDS research were unable to solve a problem for almost 10 years.	___	___
3. Scientists put the problem on the Foldit site, and gamers from the U.S. solved it in 10 weeks.	___	___
4. Today, millions of people work together in ways that weren't possible 20 years ago.	___	___

D. Discuss with a partner. Do you use sites like Wikipedia and Foldit? Would you contribute to these sites? Why or why not?

CONVERSATION

Track 2-10

A. Listen to the conversation.

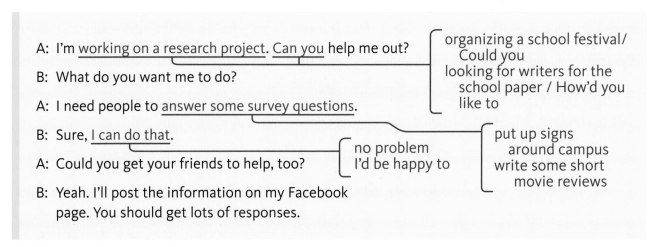

A: I'm working on a research project. Can you help me out?

B: What do you want me to do?

A: I need people to answer some survey questions.

B: Sure, I can do that.

A: Could you get your friends to help, too?

B: Yeah. I'll post the information on my Facebook page. You should get lots of responses.

    organizing a school festival / Could you

    looking for writers for the school paper / How'd you like to

    no problem / I'd be happy to

    put up signs around campus write some short movie reviews

B. Practice with a partner. Use the words on the right.

C. Practice again. Use your own ideas.

Do Your Part

▲ Leaf-cutter ants work together in the Amazon in Brazil. Ants live in colonies; some have hundreds of thousands of members.

READING

A. Predict. Look at the photo. Then read the sentences below and guess the answers.

1. Scientists believe that _____ are intelligent.

   a. individual ants   b. ant colonies   c. individual ants and ant colonies

2. Ant colonies are successful because _____ .
   a. all the ants know what's best for the group
   b. the queen is a strong leader
   c. each ant does something useful

Track 2-11

B. Read the passage. Check your ideas in **A.**

Have you ever looked at an ant and wondered how such a small creature was able to do so much? Ants travel long distances, build huge structures to live in, and sometimes even catch much larger animals to eat. For such a tiny insect, they seem quite intelligent. But according to scientists, individual ants aren't smart; ant colonies are. A group of ants can solve problems individual ants can't, such as finding food quickly or protecting their home from other insects.

In a colony, no single ant knows what's best for the group, and though there is a queen, her only role is to lay eggs; there is no group leader telling the others what to do. How is it possible, then, for the colony to get anything done? According to scientists who study ants, the colony's success is a result of *self-organizing*—each ant looking around, seeing what has to be done, and then doing its part. Perhaps this is finding food, or caring for the young, or many other tasks. Each ant has no idea that many others are doing the same thing at the same time to help the group, but it doesn't matter because the work gets done. And there's a lot, say scientists, that humans can learn from this kind of behavior.

C. Predict. What do you think humans can learn from ants' behavior? **Turn to page 122 and read the rest of the passage to check your ideas. Answer the questions there.**

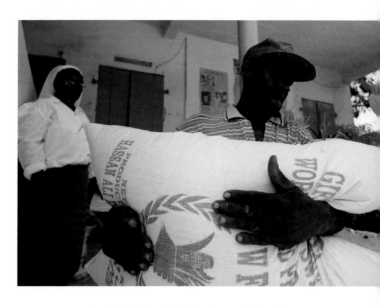

▲ The United Nations' World Food Program provides food to hungry people in countries around the globe.

LISTENING

Track 2-13

A. Listen for gist. Read the sentences below. Then listen and circle the correct answer.

The woman is asking the man to _____ .

a. donate money to a food organization
b. cook a meal for the school
c. play a game to help feed people
d. translate a website into English

Track 2-13

B. Listen for details. Are the statements below **true** or **false**? Correct the false statements.

	True	False
1. The Freerice site lets you choose from lots of subjects.	____	____
2. Users can practice and learn English vocabulary.	____	____
3. For every correct answer, you get a point.	____	____
4. There's no advertising on the website.	____	____
5. You can play alone or in teams.	____	____

C. Work with a partner. Visit the Freerice website and try the activity for five minutes with a partner. How much rice were you able to contribute? Compare results with another pair.

DISCUSSION

Persuading and negotiating. Work in pairs. **Turn to page 123** and choose one of the situations there. Ask your partner to help you. Use the language below and on page 123. Then change roles and practice again using a new situation.

> **All you have to do is** donate twenty dollars. It's for a good cause.

> **I don't know.** I don't have much money right now.

> **I understand, but** without your support . . .

> Okay, I'll tell you what I can do. I'll . . .

Citizen Scientists

▲ Albert Lin

BEFORE YOU WATCH

About the video. Dr. Albert (Yu Min) Lin is a scientist who is trying to find Genghis Khan's tomb. He is visiting the Burkhan Khaldun, a group of mountains in northern Mongolia where Genghis Khan may be buried. He is using a project called the Human Computation Network to help him. Thousands of "citizen scientist" volunteers from all over the world are also helping Dr. Lin to locate the tomb—from the comfort of their own homes.

Work with a partner. Look at the photo. Read about Genghis Khan and **About the video**. Then answer the questions with a partner.

1. Who was Genghis Khan?
2. What is Albert Lin trying to do?
3. Who is helping him and how?

For centuries, archaeologists have failed to find the tomb of Genghis Khan, the legendary Mongolian ruler. Following his death in 1227, Khan was buried in a secret location in northern Mongolia.

WHILE YOU WATCH

A. Watch the video. How does the Human Computation Network work? Complete the statements below.

1. A satellite (in space) took _____ photos of the Burkhan Khaldun region.
2. Dr. Lin's team posted the photos on a _____.
3. Citizen scientists _____ the photos on a computer.
4. The volunteers tag (mark) anything in the photos that looks _____.
5. Dr. Lin and his team examine the volunteers' tags and visit the sites.

B. Watch again. What did the citizen scientists find?

a. one of Genghis Khan's homes
b. a structure built by Genghis Khan
c. a tomb older than Genghis Khan

AFTER YOU WATCH

A. Work with a partner. Would you like to be a citizen scientist and volunteer to help find Genghis Khan's tomb? Why?

B. Work in a small group. What other projects do you think could be crowdsourced (use citizen volunteers)? Imagine a project that interests you, and answer the following questions about it:

What is the project called?　　　　　　What do participants have to do?

What does it study?　　　　　　　　　Why is it an important project?

Then tell another group about your project and try to persuade them to join in. The other group says if they want to participate and why or why not.

▼ Albert Lin and his research team

85

A Worthy Cause

You are going to research a person or project to support.

A. Choose a cause to support. Work on your own.

> Research a project from one of the sites below.
> helpfromhome.org   www.kiva.org   www.kickstarter.com
> OR
> Choose a project in your community or school.

B. Prepare a presentation. Prepare a one-minute presentation. You need to explain:
a. What is the project?
b. Why is it worth supporting?

C. Present your choice. Work in a group of four. Tell the group about your chosen project. You have one minute. Close by asking for the group's help. The others should listen and take notes.

D. Decide which cause(s) to support. Your group has the equivalent of US$100 to spend, and each person has four hours a week to volunteer. How will you use this money and time to help the four candidates you learned about in **C**? Review your notes. Then negotiate with your group and make a plan together. Share your decision with the class.

Look online for causes you can support in your local area.

▼ A refugee camp set up by volunteers from Venezuela after the 2010 earthquake in Haiti

THINK ABOUT THE PHOTO

A. Learn about the photo. Complete the description of the photo using the words below.

> trolley   camouflage   invisible   vegetables   supermarket   laughs

> A woman **1.** _____ as she pushes her shopping **2.** _____
> past the Chinese artist Liu Bolin. Liu Bolin used paint to **3.** _____ himself
> and blend in with the **4.** _____ on the shelves of a
> **5.** _____ in Beijing. Liu is also known as the "Vanishing Artist." He started
> his art of becoming **6.** _____ more than six years ago.

B. Look at the photo. Think of a title. Then share your title with the class.
Vote on the best one.

_____

DISCUSSION

A. Learn more online. Do an Internet search to find out more about Liu Bolin's art.

B. Share your information. Tell your partner what you found out.

C. Discuss with a partner.

1. What do you like or dislike about Liu Bolin's art?

2. Where do you think Liu Bolin should be photographed next?

> He could camouflage himself in front of the *Mona Lisa* in Paris!

CAPTION COMPETITION

What is Liu Bolin thinking?
Tell a partner.

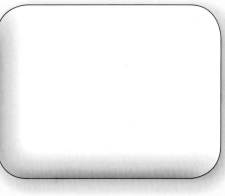

Artist Liu Bolin camouflaged
at a supermarket in Beijing

Review 4

A. Vocabulary review. Complete each sentence using the words in the box.

> thought-provoking   colony   vandalism   absolutely   collaborating

1. This sculpture is _____ amazing.
2. Many people think that graffiti is just _____.
3. I loved that installation. It was really _____.
4. What do you think about _____ together on the next project?
5. Painter Hans Hoffman started an artist's _____, where artists can work together and learn from each other.

B. Questions and answers. Draw lines to match the questions to the answers.

1. What do you think of this picture? •   • a. No, I'm planning to go next week.
2. Have you seen the new art •   • b. It depends on what you want me to do.
   exhibition in town?
                                                • c. Well, two heads are better than one!
3. What do you think about •
   collaborating with me on this?   • d. I just don't get it.
4. Have you ever donated money? •   • e. Yeah, I always give something if there
                                                     is a big disaster in the world.
5. Can you help me out? •

C. Complete the questions with your own idea. Then interview your partner.

1. What do you think about _____?   3. Have you seen _____ yet?
2. How do you feel about _____?   4. What kind of _____ do you like?

D. Work with a partner. Try to persuade your partner to do one of the following. Then swap.

- help you with your homework
- give you some money
- join a club
- go somewhere together
- your idea _____

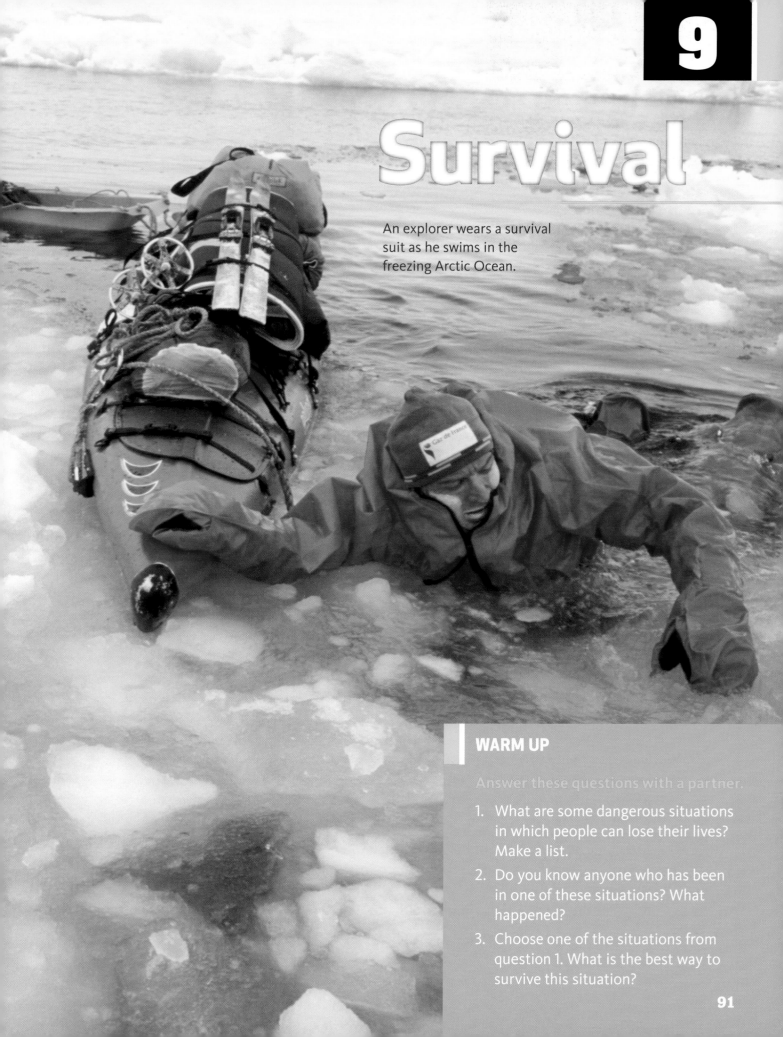

9

Survival

An explorer wears a survival suit as he swims in the freezing Arctic Ocean.

Answer these questions with a partner.

1. What are some dangerous situations in which people can lose their lives? Make a list.

2. Do you know anyone who has been in one of these situations? What happened?

3. Choose one of the situations from question 1. What is the best way to survive this situation?

RESCUED!

▲ A container ship sinks after breaking in two during a storm.

Nigeria

LISTENING

A. Predict. Look at the photos above and on the right. What do you think happened to Harrison Okene?

Track 2-14 **B. Listen for gist.** You will hear a news story. Read **a–c** below. Listen and choose the best title for the news story you hear.

a. Man Swims to Safety After Ship Sinks
b. Man Rescues Crewmates Trapped Underwater
c. Man Survives Underwater for Three Days

Track 2-14 **C. Listen for details.** Read the summary below. Then listen again and underline any information that is NOT correct. At the end, correct the false information.

On the morning of May 26, Harrison Okene woke up because he was hungry. His ship was traveling through stormy seas near Nigeria when, suddenly, a huge wave hit the boat and it sank. Okene was trapped inside the ship, but he survived by swimming to a small room that wasn't completely filled with water. He had no food and only one bottle of fresh water to drink.

After almost three hours underwater, Okene was rescued by a South African diving team. They knew he was alive and were trying to find him. The team took Okene to the surface immediately. Okene says the experience scared him, but he hopes to work on a ship again one day in the future.

D. Discuss with a partner. Take turns retelling Harrison Okene's story in your own words. Did Okene survive because he was prepared or because he was lucky?

CONVERSATION

A. Listen to the conversation.

A: Did you hear about <u>the guy who was fishing near Mexico</u>?

> the teenage girl in the U.S. who fell 1,000 meters
> the guy who got lost in the jungle in Borneo

B: No, what happened?

A: <u>His small boat got lost in the Pacific. When he was found a year later, he was almost 9,700 kilometers away from Mexico</u>!

> She was skydiving and her parachute didn't open, but she lived
> An orangutan found him and led him back to camp

B: Wait, <u>are you saying that he survived for a year in a small boat on the Pacific Ocean</u>?

> do you mean that she fell from a plane and survived
> so you're telling me that he was saved by a wild animal

A: Yeah, can you believe it?

B: No, that's incredible!

B. Practice with a partner. Use the words on the right.

C. Practice again. Talk about an interesting survival or rescue story you know about, or research one online. Tell three different classmates your story, and listen to theirs. Which story is the most incredible?

▲ Harrison Okene underwater on the ship he worked on as a cook

◄ Harrison Okene back home. He never wants to work on a ship again.

93

READING

A. Predict. Look at the photo and read the first paragraph in the passage. What is the passage about?

 B. Read the rest of the story. Put the events in order from **1–7**. Then listen and check your answers.

Track 2-16

SURVIVING A CRISIS

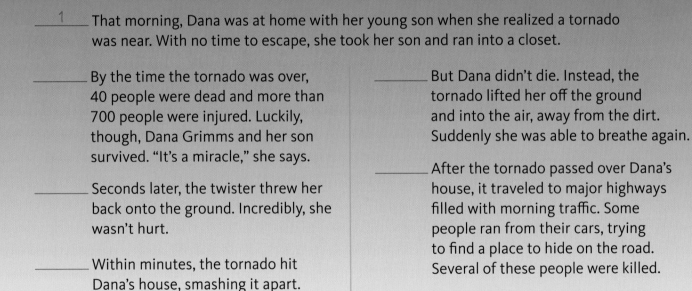

Oklahoma City

6:25 A.M.—A large tornado touches down in Oklahoma City. It's almost a kilometer and a half wide, and its winds are moving at 512 kilometers per hour, the fastest tornado ever documented. It's destroying everything in its path and it's moving toward the home of Dana Grimms.

___1___ That morning, Dana was at home with her young son when she realized a tornado was near. With no time to escape, she took her son and ran into a closet.

_____ By the time the tornado was over, 40 people were dead and more than 700 people were injured. Luckily, though, Dana Grimms and her son survived. "It's a miracle," she says.

_____ Seconds later, the twister threw her back onto the ground. Incredibly, she wasn't hurt.

_____ Within minutes, the tornado hit Dana's house, smashing it apart. Strong winds blew dust and dirt everywhere. Dana inhaled so much dirt that she couldn't breathe. She thought she was going to die.

_____ But Dana didn't die. Instead, the tornado lifted her off the ground and into the air, away from the dirt. Suddenly she was able to breathe again.

_____ After the tornado passed over Dana's house, it traveled to major highways filled with morning traffic. Some people ran from their cars, trying to find a place to hide on the road. Several of these people were killed.

_____ Dana stayed on the ground until the twister passed. Nearby, she found her son. He was also unhurt.

C. Work with a partner. Student A: Take the role of Dana. **Student B:** You are a news reporter. Use the questions below to interview Student A.

1. Before the tornado hit, where were you? Why didn't you escape?
2. During the storm, did you think you might die? Why? What saved you?
3. After the storm, you said your survival was a miracle. What did you mean?

D. Change roles. Student A: You are a news reporter. Interview your partner using questions **1** and **2** above. **Student B:** You are a person who was in traffic on the morning of the tornado.

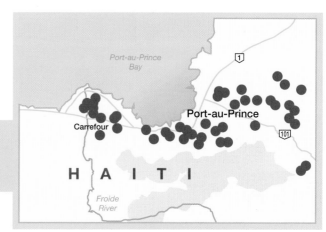

LISTENING

Patrick Meier creates online crisis maps that show where help is most needed in an emergency. Meier created one of these maps to help people in an earthquake in Port-au-Prince, Haiti.

A. Work with a partner. What does Patrick Meier do?

 B. Listen for gist. Number the questions (**1–3**) in the order Patrick Meier answers them. You will hear only his three answers, not the questions.

_____ Did the map help at all?

_____ When an emergency like an earthquake happens, what do rescuers need to know?

_____ After the earthquake in Haiti, how did you get information to create a crisis map?

 C. Listen for details. How does Meier answer questions **1–3**? Read the answer choices. Then listen and circle the correct answers. Sometimes more than one answer is possible.

1. It's important to understand (**where the people in need are / who needs help / why there is a lack of water**).
2. People in Port-au-Prince (**posted information on Twitter / wrote letters to Meier / sent text messages asking for help**).
3. (**Yes, it saved hundreds of lives. / A little, but hundreds still died. / No, not this time.**)

DISCUSSION

Narrating a story. Tell a story about an emergency you or someone you know experienced. Your story can be real or made up. Using the language below, explain when and where it happened, and what happened before, during, and after the event. The group will listen and ask questions. At the end, each person should say if you are telling a real story or not.

Prior to / Before the storm . . .

I waited until the storm was over.

During the storm . . .

After / Once it was over . . .

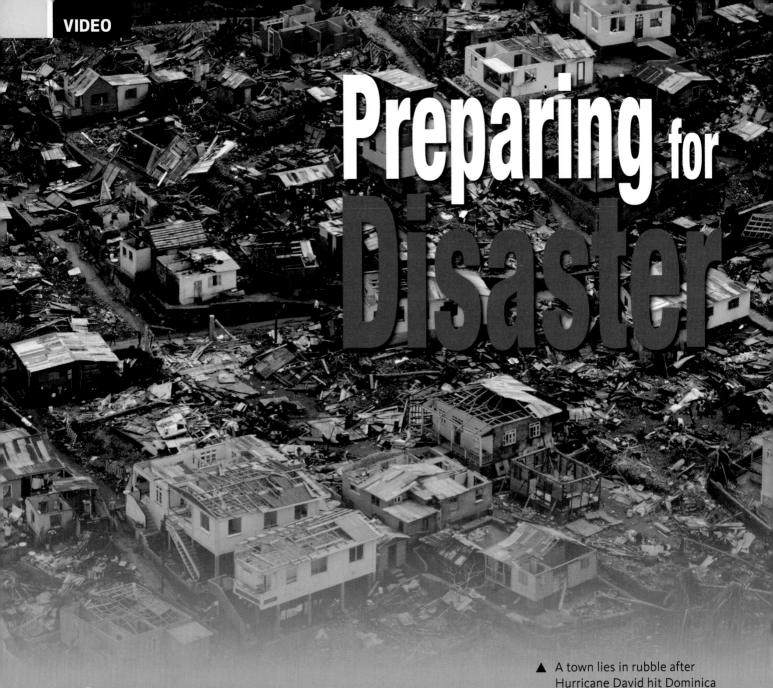

Preparing for Disaster

▲ A town lies in rubble after Hurricane David hit Dominica

BEFORE YOU WATCH

About the video. Aton Edwards is the author of the book "Preparedness Now: An Emergency Survival Guide." To prepare for a major disaster (e.g., a big earthquake), he says there are things people can do. In the video, he talks about what these things are.

A. Work with a partner. Read **About the video**. Answer the questions.

1. Who is Aton Edwards? What does he teach people to do?

2. What are some examples of major disasters? How likely are they to happen in your city or country?

B. Predict. Work with a partner. Choose one of the major disasters above. What advice might Aton Edwards give people to help them prepare for it? Make a list of ten things you need.

WHILE YOU WATCH

A. Watch the video. What does Edwards carry in his survival kit? Check the items he carries. How many of them were in your list in **Before You Watch**?

☐ a pry bar to open windows and doors
☐ a first aid kit, with band-aids and medicines
☐ a knife for protection against wild animals
☐ a bag of toiletries, with soap and toothpaste
☐ a water container

☐ an axe for cutting down trees
☐ instant food
☐ cooking tools
☐ a rope ladder for escaping from tall buildings
☐ a tent

B. Watch again. You will hear sentences **1–4** below in the video. What do the words in **blue** mean? Choose **a** or **b**.

1. Aton Edwards says, "The survivor of the future is **mobile**."
   a. able to move from place to place   b. careful to stay in one safe place

2. Aton Edwards says, "If you think you can **hunker down** in one area, you're wrong."
   a. stay in one place   b. move around freely

3. "In the event of a major disaster . . . your everyday routine would **cease to exist**," believes Edwards.
   a. be very difficult   b. end

4. At the end, the narrator says, "Those who are **flexible** . . . will be the successful survivors."
   a. adaptable, able to change easily   b. healthy and fit

AFTER YOU WATCH

Talk with a partner. Discuss the questions.

1. Do you agree with Edwards' advice about surviving a disaster? Why or why not?

2. Surviving a difficult situation often depends on a person's attitude. Check the qualities you need in order to survive difficult situations.

☐ brave   ☐ calm   ☐ careful   ☐ determined
☐ flexible / adaptable   ☐ optimistic / positive   ☐ organized   ☐ lucky

3. Do you think Aton Edwards has these qualities? Do you? Give an example from your life.

Aton Edwards teaching ▶
survival skills to a
group of people

WHAT'S YOUR PLAN?

A public service announcement (PSA) is a TV, radio, or Internet advertisement with a message. You will make a PSA that explains how to survive an event.

A. Choose an idea. With a partner, choose a survival situation from the box below.

SURVIVAL SITUATIONS

- a natural emergency (a fire, a big earthquake)
- a blackout (no electricity for many days)
- a very serious weather event
- your idea: _____

B. Prepare your PSA. In pairs, research and prepare a two-minute PSA. You can make a poster, a radio announcement, or a video. The PSA should explain what to do before, during, and after the event. Explain why each step is important.

C. Write a quiz. Prepare a short multiple-choice quiz about the situation. **See page 124 for an example.**

D. Present your PSA to another pair. Pair 1: Give the other pair your quiz. Then present your PSA. **Pair 2:** Take the quiz. Then listen to the other pair's PSA. Check your answers. On a scale of 1 (*not prepared at all*) to 4 (*very prepared*), how ready were you for the event? Then change roles.

A survival kit ▼

Look online for facts and figures to use in your PSA.

Innovation

10

A rotating boat lift connecting
canals in Falkirk, Scotland

WARM UP

Answer these questions with a partner.

1. What are some inventions that have improved
   people's lives in the last 10 to 15 years?

2. Which of these inventions do you think will
   still be used in another 10 to 15 years?

3. In the future, which jobs will still have to
   be done by people? Why?

99

Useful Technology

▲ Twelve-year-old Leon McCarthy was born without fingers on his left hand. His new hand is made of parts printed from a 3-D printer.

LISTENING

A. Predict. You will hear someone talk about 3-D printers. Read the four questions below. Can you guess any of the answers?

_____ Is 3-D printing fast?	_____ What can you make with a 3-D printer?
_____ What exactly is a 3-D printer?	_____ Can anyone buy and use a 3-D printer?

Track 2-18 **B. Listen for gist.** In **A**, number the questions **1–4** in the order the speaker answers them. You will hear only the answers, not the questions.

Track 2-18 **C. Listen for details.** Below are answers to questions **1–4**. For each pair, circle the correct answer.

1. a. It creates physical objects.
   b. It prints on special paper.
	3. a. No, it takes a long time.
	   b. Yes, it works very quickly.

2. a. a full-sized car
   b. human body parts
	4. a. No, they're sold only to companies.
	   b. Yes, anyone can buy them, but they can be expensive.

D. Discuss with a partner. Do you think 3-D printers are useful? Why or why not? How else might 3-D printers be used in the future?

CONVERSATION

Track 2-19

A. Listen to the conversation.

A: This is an interesting invention. It's called Ring.

> Google Glass
> the Emotiv EEG

B: What is it?

A: It's a ring that lets you control things by moving your finger.

> wearable computer / looks like a pair of glasses
> headset / reads your brainwaves

B: What exactly does it do?

A: A lot of things. For example, you can use it to turn off the lights, write a text, or even pay your bills.

> take photos or video and surf the Internet
> move objects on a computer screen with your mind

B: It sounds like a useful tool.

B. Practice with a partner. Use the words on the right.

C. Practice again. Talk about other inventions you know, or do a search online for new inventions. What can you do with each? Are they useful? Why or why not?

▼ A man uses the Emotiv EEG to control a toy with his brain

READING

A. Predict. Look at the photo and read the first paragraph of the reading. What problem will the passage talk about? Is this a problem where you live? Can you think of some possible solutions to this problem?

Track 2-20

B. Read the passage. Check your ideas in **A**.

THE FUTURE OF CARS

THE PROBLEM: Every year the average commuter spends about 34 hours in traffic. Not only does this cause people to lose time each day, it wastes gas, creates pollution, and leads to higher costs for goods if they're delayed by heavy traffic.

A POSSIBLE SOLUTION: As city populations worldwide continue to grow, more people are driving than ever before. Urban planners are looking for solutions for the problem. Some believe the answer is to make streets wider and highways bigger. However, studies show that when streets become wider, all that happens is that more cars come onto the roads, worsening the problem. Other studies confirm that traffic is rarely caused by too few roads or by streets that are too narrow. Researchers have found that the main cause of many traffic jams is human decision-making. Thousands of cars on the same road means thousands of individual drivers making different choices: How fast should I go? Which street should I drive on? How far should I stay from the car in front of me? With this in mind, urban planners—and car makers—are now exploring another option in order to reduce traffic: driverless cars.

HOW THEY WORK: How will these cars work? The idea is simple: Instead of being driven by a person, they'll be driven by a computer. The car will make decisions about speed, keeping a safe distance, and which roads to take. It will also interact with other cars' computers to help it make the best driving decisions. Car companies like Toyota, Audi, and BMW are already working on driverless cars, and some experts predict that in the next decade or two, most cars in major cities worldwide will be driverless.

C. Reading comprehension. Answer the questions below with a partner.

1. What is the main cause of traffic problems in cities?
2. What solution do some urban planners think might fix the problem?
3. How will this invention work?
4. Do experts think this solution will be popular?

▼ During rush hour in many cities, it can take commuters hours to go a short distance.

LISTENING

A. Predict. What are some possible advantages and disadvantages of using a driverless car? Tell a partner.

B. Listen for gist. You will hear four different speakers give their opinions about driverless cars. Is each speaker mostly positive (**+**) or negative (**−**) about these cars? Circle **+** or **−** in the chart below.

Track 2-21

▲ A driverless car drives itself through Washington, D.C., U.S.A.

Speaker	Opinion	Reason
1	+ −	a. You can do other things during your morning _____ . b. You can go places _____ . c. Roads will be _____ .
2	+ −	a. Taxi and truck drivers and delivery people will _____ their _____ .
3	+ −	a. A driverless car can _____ itself. b. It can save you _____ .
4	+ −	a. The car's computer could stop _____ . b. It would be easy to break into and _____ a driverless car.

C. Listen for details. What reasons do the speakers give for their opinions? Complete each sentence with one or two words.

Track 2-21

DISCUSSION

Giving several reasons. What do you think of driverless cars? Will they mostly improve people's lives or cause more problems? Use at least two reasons from **Listening B** and research others online to explain your answer to a partner. Use the language below.

> A driverless car will **not only** be faster, it'll **also** be safer. **Plus**, it'll be easier to . . .

> I'm not really sure the car would be safe. **For one thing**, the computer could stop working. **And what's more** . . .

CLEVER MACHINES

◀ Robot waiters at a restaurant in Harbin, China

BEFORE YOU WATCH

About the video. Robotics expert Chad Jenkins says that recent advances in technology will soon make robots a bigger part of everyday life. In the near future, these machines will help us perform more tasks in our homes and workplaces. But first, they have a lot to learn.

A. Work with a partner. Read **About the video**. Then read the questions below and try to guess the answers.

1. What are some ways that humans use robots now?

2. Why aren't we using robots more in our daily lives now?

3. How might they be used more in the future?

B. Predict. How do you think scientists teach robots to do things?

WHILE YOU WATCH

A. Watch the video. Check your answers in **Before You Watch.**

B. Watch again. Read **1–3** below. Then watch again and choose the correct answers.

1. There are different ways you can teach a robot to do something. Choose the three you see and hear about in the video.

    ☐ You talk to it.
    ☐ You use a remote control device.
    ☐ You move its arm.
    ☐ You play a game with it.
    ☐ It watches you and copies your actions.

2. Near the end of the video, Chad Jenkins uses a robotic mobile device. Circle the correct answer to complete the sentence.

    With this tool you can _____ .

    a. teach other robots to do things
    b. be in two places at one time
    c. help the elderly and disabled

AFTER YOU WATCH

Talk with a partner. Discuss the questions. Then compare your answers with another pair.

1. What are some ways Jenkins' robotic device could be used at your school, your workplace, or your home?

2. Does Chad Jenkins think robots will improve our lives in the future? Do you? Why or why not?

3. South Korea hopes to have a robot in every home by 2020, and the government is working to create a list of guidelines (rules) about how these machines can and cannot be used. Think of 3–4 rules you'd include. Explain your reasons for each rule.

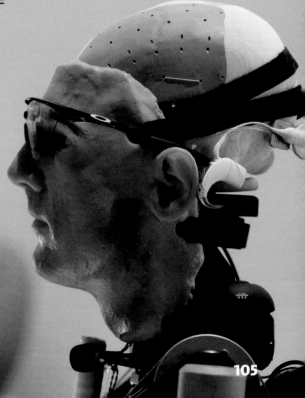

▼ Rex, a two-meter-tall artificial human at a science museum in London, England

A USEFUL INVENTION

You are going to come up with a new invention and research it.

A. Think about simple inventions. Read the information below. Can you think of other simple inventions that have improved people's lives? Complete this sentence with your ideas: *In the past . . . Then . . .*

> A number of problems in daily life have been solved by simple inventions. For example, in the past, it was expensive to make long-distance phone calls. Then services like Skype made it possible to call people for free using a computer.

B. Identify a problem. Work with a partner. Think of an existing problem that needs to be fixed. Then invent something to solve the problem. Answer these questions:

Search for "future inventions" online for some ideas.

- Who does your invention help?
- What does it do? How does it work?
- How does it improve people's lives?
- What would you call it?

C. Present your invention. Prepare an advertisement for your invention. It can be a video, poster, or a slideshow. Then, join two other pairs and present your advertisement. When you listen to the other presentations, think about the questions below:

1. Would you use the product? Why?

2. Is there anything you'd change about the product?

D. Give feedback to other inventors.
Tell the other inventors your answers to **C**.

A robot named "Robovie-II," developed in Japan, ▶ is designed to help elderly people.

THINK ABOUT THE PHOTO

A. Complete the description. Complete the information about the photo on the next page, using the words in the box.

> stored   tower   plant   increase   conveyor   automatically

A car is pictured in a delivery **1.** _____ at Volkswagen's company headquarters in Germany. The cars are built in the car **2.** _____ next to the headquarters. They are then transported by **3.** _____ belt and **4.** _____ in one of two towers. Customers can go directly to the headquarters and watch their new cars being delivered to them **5.** _____.

B. Think of a title for this photo. Then share your title with the class and vote on the best one.

_____

_____

DISCUSSION

A. Find out more information. Do an Internet search to find out more about the car towers.

B. Share your information. Tell your partner what you found out about them.

C. Discuss with a partner. What do you think is innovative about the car delivery towers?

CAPTION COMPETITION

What do you think Fabian Bimmer, the photographer, was thinking when he took the photograph? Tell a partner.

Two Volkswagen cars are carried in a delivery tower at the company's headquarters.

Review 5

A. Vocabulary review. Complete the conversation with vocabulary from Unit 9.

A: Did you **1.** _____ about the guy who was attacked by a crocodile?

B: No, what **2.** _____?

A: Well, **3.** _____ a fishing trip, a crocodile appeared on shore and tried to bite the man. But the man attacked the crocodile instead.

B: **4.** _____, are you saying the man fought back?

A: Yeah, can you **5.** _____ it? He poked the crocodile in the eye with his thumb and the crocodile went away.

B: Wow, that's incredible!

B. Complete the definitions with words from Unit 10.

1. An _____ is a person who creates new things.

2. A _____ is a machine that creates a solid object from a digital model.

3. A _____ is a person who travels to work and home again.

4. An _____ is a person who manages city and suburban areas and thinks about how to best use the land and roads, etc.

5. An _____ is a person who knows a lot about something or has a lot of skill in a certain field.

C. Tell a story. Tell a story to your partner about something that happened to you. It could be a funny story, a scary story, a dramatic story, a happy story, or a sad story.

D. Make a list of five new inventions. Work with a partner. Ask your partner what he or she thinks of each invention?

What do you think of having a home solar panel system?

I think it's a great idea. If I had solar panels, it would make my monthly electricity bill a lot cheaper!

TARGET VOCABULARY

An **acquaintance** is someone you have met but don't know well.

A **close friend** or **best friend** is someone you know well and like a lot.

A **companion** is a friend or someone you spend time with.

If you **energize** someone, you give them energy to do something.

If you **get together** with someone, you meet the person in order to do something.

If you **hang out** with someone, you spend time together.

If you have an **open mind** or are **open minded**, you are willing to consider other people's ideas and opinions.

If you **keep in touch** with someone, you continue to email, phone, or see the person.

IMPORTANT LANGUAGE

Describing similarities and differences
My best friend Jin and I . . .
• **have a lot in common.** = We are very similar.
• **are kind of similar.** = We are a little bit similar.
• **are completely / totally different.** = We are very different.

Jin and I are different. He's **older / nicer** than I am.	Add *-er* or *-r* to most one syllable adjectives. Notice that *than* follows the adjective.
I'm **quieter** than he is. He's **friendlier** than I am. I'm **more patient / thoughtful** than he is. He's **more outgoing** than I am.	Add *-r* or *-er* to adjectives with two syllables that end in an unstressed syllable. Use *more* with other two-syllable adjectives, especially those words ending with *-ed, -ful, -ing,* or *-ous,* and with adjectives that have three or more syllables.
He's good in English, but I'm **better** (than he is) in math.	The comparative of *good* is *better*.
He's **way / much** more outgoing than I am.	In informal speech, to stress that you are very different from someone, it's possible to add *way* or *much* before the comparison.

Explaining how to do something
Begin with some background:
How can you make friends at a new school? Today, my partner and I will tell you.
Then list and explain your ideas:
One way to make friends at a new school is to . . . Doing this is helpful because . . . Another way is to . . .   A third way is to . . . And finally, you can . . .

PROJECT

Make a survey. Write some survey questions to ask people about their friends. How did you meet? How do you stay friends? What makes a good friendship? Interview different people. Share your results with the class.

111

TARGET VOCABULARY

If you are **afraid** or **scared of** something, that thing makes you feel fear.

A person with **courage** isn't afraid to do something difficult or dangerous, *but you do it!* ~~I'm afraid but I do it anyway~~

If something **creeps you out**, it makes you feel ~~afraid.~~ *uncomfortable*

If you **freak out**, you act in a very nervous, emotional way.

If something **freaks you out**, it makes you feel very nervous or scared.

If something you do is a **risk**, it can be dangerous. *take a chance*

If something is **risky**, it is dangerous. *adj*

A **risk-taker** is a person who likes to do dangerous things. */chance of a bad result*

A **thrill** is a feeling of excitement. *thrilling /thrilled (adj)*

If something is **thrilling**, it's very exciting.

If an event is **traumatizing**, it is very scary, upsetting, and shocking. *maybe for a long time.* *trama crewzing*

IMPORTANT LANGUAGE

Talking about things that scare you	
I'm afraid / scared of dogs. the dark. going to the dentist. speaking in public.	*Be afraid / scared of* is followed by a noun. This can be one word (*dogs*), a noun phrase (*the dark*), or a gerund (**going** to the dentist, **speaking** in public, **watching** scary movies).
During her presentation, she **freaked out** and started talking too fast.	*Freak out* is a phrasal verb (a verb + particle with two or three words).
Going to the dentist **freaks** <u>me</u> **out**. Spiders **creep** <u>him</u> **out**.	It's possible to separate some phrasal verbs, like *freak out* and *creep out*. Notice that the <u>pronoun</u> always goes in the middle.

Making and responding to suggestions	

Every time I give a presentation, I get nervous.
   Try memorizing your speech.
   Try to memorize your speech.
   Try not to worry.
I'm not sure if that'll work.
Good idea. I'll give it a try.
	To make a polite suggestion, use *try* + gerund (*memorizing*) or infinitive (*to memorize*).
	
	If you want to tell someone not to do something, use *try* + *not* + infinitive.

Help! There's a tarantula on my back!
   Try not to move!
   Don't move!
	In an emergency, people are more direct.

PROJECT

Keep a research diary. Make a list of your fears. Choose one fear. Plan strategies about how to overcome that fear. Keep a diary about what happens. Make a movie or poster presentation and share your results with the class.

READING

Track 1-13

B. Split reading. Student B: Read the passage below. Then answer the questions in the chart, under "Student B."

C. Work in pairs: Ask your partner the questions in the chart. Write his or her answers under "Student A." Then turn back to page 34.

	Student A	Student B
1. What are scientists studying?		*Special groups of people around the world.*
2. What have they learned?		*learn how special genes work could help extend life for us all and keep us healthier too.*

LIVING TO
120+
These babies may live to be 120, thanks to new discoveries in science.

How long can humans live? In most developed countries, people are now living an average of 75 years. But scientists are trying to find ways to lengthen our lives—perhaps to 120 years or older—and to help us remain young as we age.

To do this, scientists are studying special groups of people around the world. These people seem to be immune to certain diseases that shorten our lives. Some Ecuadorians, for example, have a gene that seems to prevent dangerous diseases like cancer and diabetes. Japanese American men also seem to have a special gene that lowers their chance of getting cancer and heart disease. Learning how these genes work could help extend life for us all and keep us healthier, too.

TARGET VOCABULARY

- Your **diet** is the type of food that you regularly eat. *(what do you eat)*
- Our **genes** control our physical characteristics, growth, and development. Genes form long strings called DNA.
- If you **prevent** something from happening, you stop it or make sure it does not happen. *(stop before something happens)*
- If something **relieves** an unpleasant feeling, it stops or lessens the feeling. *(stop a bad feeling)*
- A **virus** is a kind of germ that can cause disease. *(illness (n) / sickness (n))*

IMPORTANT LANGUAGE

Common health problems
have a(n) cold, cough, earache, fever, hangover, headache, sore throat, stomach ache, toothache, upset stomach *(food almost come up)* *(back ache)*   **have the** flu *(hurt / pain)*   **have** allergies, laryngitis, insomnia *(can't speak   can't sleep)*

Making suggestions and giving advice	
I have a sore throat. 　You **should / ought to** go home and rest. 　**Why don't you** go home and rest?	Use **you should / ought to . . .** or **why don't you . . . + the base form of the verb** to make suggestions or give advice.

Introducing an opinion and disagreeing politely
In my opinion, / **If you ask me,** living to 120 sounds great. *(If I'm healthy)*
Really? I completely disagree. For one thing . . . *(example / idea)*   **I know what you mean, but** / **I know what you're saying, but** living longer doesn't mean living better. *(however)*

(→ I see. / I understand. I got it.)

PROJECT

Research a health issue. Choose a health issue (e.g. *We should eat less junk food*) different from the one you did in the **Expansion Activity**. Use the Internet to find evidence to support your ideas. Present your results to the class.

READING

Track 1-18

B. Split reading. Student B: Read the text below.

C. Work in pairs. Ask your partner questions to help you answer the questions below.

1. How old is Kalash culture? How many Kalash people did there use to be? How many are there today?
2. Why could the Kalash language easily die out?
3. How is Sayed Gul Kalash trying to preserve Kalash culture?
4. The number of Kalash people is decreasing. What is causing this change?

A Disappearing Culture

In Northern Pakistan, near the Afghan border, there is a group of people called the Kalasha. Once powerful and widespread, the Kalash civilization once had tens of thousands of people; today, there are only about 3,500. In just a few generations, this culture, which is over 3,000 years old, may disappear.

Sayed Gul Kalash, a member of this community, is working hard to save her language and culture from extinction, but it won't be easy. In an increasingly globalized and connected world, languages like Mandarin and English, Russian and Hindi, Spanish and Arabic dominate. Parents in small villages often encourage their children to move away from their language and culture and toward those that will help them be more successful in life. Today, numbers are decreasing as more and more Kalash children are being educated in mainstream schools, and more people are moving away and marrying outside the Kalash culture. "It's understandable," says Sayed Gul Kalash. But she reminds us that every culture is unique and has value. When one culture is lost, we all lose something.

TARGET VOCABULARY

If you **adapt** to a new situation, you change your behavior so you can deal with the new situation successfully.

If something **disappears**, it no longer exists.

If a person or thing **dominates** another, they have more power than the other thing.

If something is **endangered**, it is in danger of dying out completely.

If something is **mainstream**, it is normal or the most common. A *mainstream school*, for example, is the type of school most people go to.

The **middle class** is a group of people in society. They are not poor or rich. They are in the middle.

If you try to **preserve** something, you try to save or protect it.

If you **resist** something (like a change), you refuse to accept it.

IMPORTANT LANGUAGE

Talking about the past with *used to*	
Mario **used to** live in a small town, but he doesn't anymore. Today, he lives in Mexico City. He **didn't use to** own a car, but he does now.	Speakers use *used to* to talk about things that happened in the past regularly, or for a period of time, but don't anymore.

Making predictions and talking about consequences with *if*		
if-clause	*Result clause*	
If the Kalash **train** more local teachers,	children **will learn** their language and culture.	Use this form of the conditional to make predictions and talk about possible future consequences.
If the children only **learn** their own language,	they **may / might not get** good jobs in the future.	In the result clause, it's also possible to use modals like *may* and *might (not)* to make predictions and talk about consequences.

PROJECT

Interview people about change. Interview people about some changes happening in your city or country. What are the consequences of the changes for these people? Do they think the change is positive or negative? Make a video or presentation about the people. Share your presentation with the class.

UNIT 5 SUCCESS

TARGET VOCABULARY

An **accomplishment** or **achievement** is something you succeed in doing, especially after a lot of hard work.

If you have **connections**, you know the right people who can help you.

Determination is the desire to keep going and never quit.

If you **give up**, you decide you cannot do something and you stop doing it.

A **goal** is something you hope to do. If you achieve a goal, you do or get what you wanted.

A person with **good looks** is attractive.

If you have **good luck**, you are successful and good things happen to you without a lot of effort.

Intelligence is the ability to think and learn things quickly and well.

If you **overcome** a problem, you successfully deal with it and control it.

Self-confidence is belief in yourself.

Adjectives to describe people: connected, determined, educated, goal-oriented, good looking, hard-working, intelligent, lucky, self-confident

IMPORTANT LANGUAGE

<table>
<tr><td colspan="3" align="center">Talking about goals</td></tr>
<tr><td rowspan="2">One of my goals is to visit Europe</td><td>soon/ this summer / this term / next month.</td><td>A short-term goal is something you want to do soon.</td></tr>
<tr><td>after graduation / next year / in 2020 / someday / at some point.</td><td>A long-term goal is something you want to do later in the future.</td></tr>
</table>

PROJECT

Collect stories about success. Collect stories from different people about times they have been successful, or times they have learned from failure. Share the most interesting stories with the class.

Giving a presentation
Start your presentation
My nomination for [the lifetime achievement award] is . . .
Explain your reasons
Let me tell you a little about [name of person] and why I chose him/her. First of all . . . ; in addition . . . ; also . . . ; and finally . . . .
End your presentation
For these reasons, I hope you will nominate . . . for [this year's lifetime achievement award].

TARGET VOCABULARY

A **consumer** is a person who buys things.

Consumerism is the belief that it is good to buy lots of things.

Consumption is the act of buying and using things.

Goods are things that are made to be sold.

If a country **exports** goods, it sends them to another country.

Imported goods come into your country from another country.

If something is made or grown **locally**, it is made or grown in your area.

If you **manufacture** a product, you make it. A **manufacturer** is a maker of something.

If you **purchase** something, you buy it.

If you **repair** something, you fix it.

If something is broken and you **replace** it, you get a new one.

Stuff is an informal way of saying "things."

IMPORTANT LANGUAGE

Talking about preferences
On Fridays, **I prefer** to bike to school (**rather than** drive).   On Fridays, **I prefer** biking to driving.
Would you rather own a bike or a car?   **I'd rather** own a bike (**than** a car).
Would you rather bike or drive to school?   **I'd rather** bike to school (**than** drive).

The passive	
Simple present	Most coffee in this country **is imported** from Brazil or Vietnam.
Simple past	I bought these boots in London, but they **were made** in Turkey.
Present perfect	Millions of acres in the Amazon have **been cut down** to raise beef.

PROJECT

Research everyday products. Make a list of products that are eco-friendly and a list of products that are environmentally unfriendly. Research ways that companies could improve environmentally unfriendly products. Make a poster or brochure to share your eco-friendly ideas with the class.

Survey. Take the survey and get your score. When you are done, turn to page 60 and do **Lesson A**.

What kind of consumer are you?

1. When an item (like a phone or printer) breaks, I prefer to _____ it.

   a. repair
   b. replace

2. I'd rather buy a product that _____ .

   a. is good for the environment, even if I have to pay more money for it

   b. costs less, even if it isn't good for the environment

3. When I go shopping, I prefer to _____ for my purchases.

   a. bring my own bags
   b. get a new bag

4. I prefer to drink _____ water.

   a. tap
   b. bottled

5. I _____ eat beef or chicken.

   a. rarely or never
   b. regularly

6. I _____ buy imported food or drinks.

   a. rarely or never
   b. regularly

7. I'd rather own a _____ .

   a. bike
   b. car

8. I'd rather live in a _____ house.

   a. small or medium-sized
   b. large

My score: _____

Now give each answer a point: a = 2 points   b = 1 point

The higher your total score, the better your purchasing choices are for the environment. The highest score possible is 16.

TARGET VOCABULARY

Abstract art uses shapes or colors rather than showing people or things.
Graffiti are words or pictures that people draw or paint on public buildings or transportation.
Pop art is a type of art that started in the 1960s. It often uses bright colors and takes
  a lot of its subject matter from everyday life.
If a person has **talent** or is **talented**, he or she has a natural ability to do something very well.
Vandalism is the act of deliberately damaging things, usually public property.

IMPORTANT LANGUAGE

Using descriptive language	
This painting (drawing / sculpture / installation / photograph / mural / video) is . . .	
amazing, awesome, beautiful, colorful, cool, fun, incredible, interesting, original/unique, realistic/life-like, terrific.	These adjectives all have a **positive** meaning.
awful/horrible/terrible, boring, depressing/dark, offensive, scary, silly, ugly, weird.	These adjectives all have a **negative** meaning.
just okay / nothing special.	Use these words to say that something is **okay** (neither great nor terrible).

This spider sculpture is **very** / **really** cool. Really? I think it's **a bit** / **kind of** / **sort of** scary. This is a **really** weird painting. Yeah, but it's also **kind of** fun.	The words in **bold** can come before an adjective. *Very* and *really* make those words stronger. *A bit, kind of*, and *sort of* are used to soften adjectives.

Saying you like, dislike, or don't understand something
What do you think of this painting?   **I love it!**   **I'm not really into** abstract art. = I don't really like (abstract art).   **I'm so over** abstract art. = I'm bored or tired of (abstract art). I don't like it anymore.   **I don't get it.** = I don't understand it.

PROJECT

Make a video documentary. Choose a different artist. Find out information about him or her. Make a short video documentary to explain about the artist's life and work. Include photos of the artist's work in your video.

READING

Track 2-12
C. Read the rest of the passage. Read the paragraph below and answer the questions that follow.

Do Your Part

▲ Townspeople working together to stop flood waters

There's a lot ants can teach us about working together and thinking about more than ourselves to improve our communities, say scientists. For example, every day millions of people drink bottled water and then throw away the plastic containers. But imagine the difference it would make if each person recycled his or her bottle. Like an ant in the colony, each person would, in fact, contribute to the greater good, simply by doing his or her part. So the next time you're wondering if it's worth it to recycle that plastic bottle, or volunteer your time, or go and vote, think about the ants in the colony and remember this: your actions matter, even small ones, even if you don't see how.

D. Understand vocabulary. Find a word or phrase above. Then circle the correct answer in **1–3**.

1. If something is *worth it*, it is (**expensive** / **useful**) to do.

2. If something *matters*, it is (**important** / **unimportant**).

3. *The greater good* is something that will help (**some** / **many**) people.

E. Work with a partner. Discuss the questions. When you are done, turn back to page 83.

1. What can humans learn from ant colonies? Use the example of recycling to explain.

2. Re-read the last sentence in the passage. Do you agree with the author? Why or why not?

3. Give another example of how one person can contribute to the greater good.

DISCUSSION

1. You're trying to raise money for a local animal shelter. The shelter needs money or it will have to close and many animals will die. Ask for donations.

2. You volunteer for an organization that plants trees in your city. It needs people to help on the weekend; it also needs money to buy supplies.

3. Your school is having a bake sale to raise money for a festival. The school needs people to donate cookies, make decorations, and volunteer two hours to sell items on the day of the sale.

4. A middle school needs student volunteers to tutor kids in English. They're trying to prepare for the high school entrance exam and they need help on Thursdays for an hour.

TARGET VOCABULARY & IMPORTANT LANGUAGE

If you **collaborate** with another person or a group of people, you work together to do something.

A **collective** action or opinion is shared by a group of people.

If you **do** your **part**, you help toward the success of something.

If you **donate** time, money, clothes, or other items, you give these things to others for free.

A **good cause** is something that is good or helpful for society.

If you **volunteer** to do something, you offer to do it, usually for free.

Persuading and Negotiating	
I'm trying to raise money for the local animal shelter. **All you have to do is** donate $20. **Here's what I'm asking for:** a donation of $20.	Negotiations often start with one speaker **explaining what he/she wants**.
I don't know . . . / The problem is . . . I don't have any money. / I'm kind of busy these days. / I'm not very good at . . .	Sometimes, the listener will **express doubt** about the offer.
I understand, but without your support, the shelter will close. **Okay, well what about** $10 instead?	If this happens, the first speaker can **make an appeal . . .** or **suggest a new offer.**
That'll work. / I can do that. I'll tell you what I can do. I'll . . . I can't . . . , but I can . . . Does that work?	The listener might then **agree to the new offer . . .** or **suggest another offer.**

PROJECT

Help a cause for real. Run an event (for example, selling clothes) to raise money for one or more of the causes you talked about in the **Expansion Activity**. After the event, tell the class what you did, and how successful you were.

EXPANSION ACTIVITY

SURVIVAL GUIDE: HIKING IN THE WILDERNESS

Work with a partner. Could you survive in the wilderness if you got lost? Take the quiz.
Circle the correct answers. Then check your answers below.

1. Before you go, you should _____.
   a. make sure you have a GPS   b. tell someone where you're going   c. buy enough supplies

2. During the hike, you get lost. You should _____.
   a. start a fire   b. try to walk back the way you came   c. stop and wait

3. While you wait for help, the best place to stay is _____.
   a. near a river   b. in an open area   c. under some large trees

TARGET VOCABULARY

Your **attitude** is the way you think about a situation.
If you **rescue** someone from a dangerous situation, you save that person.
If you **survive** a dangerous situation like an accident or illness, you do not die.
If you are **trapped** somewhere, you are unable to escape because something is stopping you.

IMPORTANT LANGUAGE

Describing a process with adverbial phrases and clauses	
Before the storm (hits), go shopping for supplies. **Prior to** the storm, go shopping for supplies.	What to do before something happens.
During the storm, stay indoors. Don't go outside **until** the storm is over. Don't go outside **until** the end.	What to do when something is happening.
After the storm, call for help if you smell gas. **After / Once** the storm is over, call for help if you smell gas.	What to do when something is finished.
The words *after*, *before*, and *until* can be followed by a noun phrase (e.g., *the storm*) or a clause (e.g., *the storm hits*). The words *during* and *prior to* are only followed by a noun or noun phrase.	

Paraphrasing to ask for clarification
Are you saying that . . . ?   Do you mean that . . . ?   So you're telling me that . . . ?

Answers: 1. a, b, c 2. a, c 3. b

PROJECT

Find out more about how people survive dangerous situations. Search online and interview people about a different survival situation. What do people do before, during, and after the event? Use the information to create a video PSA. Use words, images, and excerpts from people's interviews. When you are finished, show it to your classmates, or upload it to a video hosting website.

UNIT 10 INNOVATION

TARGET VOCABULARY

A **commuter** is someone who travels a long distance between their home and workplace every day.

An **innovation** is a new thing or a new method of doing something.

If something is **mobile**, it can be easily moved from place to place.

A **traffic jam** is a long line of vehicles that cannot move because there are too many vehicles on the road.

An **urban planner** is a person who plans the roads and organization of a city.

IMPORTANT LANGUAGE

Defining something and how it works	
What (exactly) is the Emotiv EEG? **What (exactly) does** an Emotiv EEG **do**?	Use the words and phrases in **bold** to ask what something is and to explain how it works.
It's a headset **that** reads your brainwaves. **You can use it to** move objects on a computer screen with your mind.	

Listing multiple reasons for emphasis	
A driverless car will be faster. **Plus / What's more / In addition**, it'll be easier to park.	It's common to use **these words and phrases** to add more information or list multiple points. The words in bold mean *also*.
A lot of taxi drivers will lose their jobs, **not to mention** truck drivers and delivery people. Driverless cars will be faster, **not to mention** easier to park.	*Not to mention* means *and also*.
They're using 3-D printers **not only** to make toys and jewelry, **but also** to make simple foods. A driverless car is **not only** faster, **(but)** it's **also** safer.	You can also use *not only . . . but also* to list multiple points. *Not only* and *but also* should come before similar words or phrases. When the second reason is stated as a complete sentence (*it's also safer*), you don't need *but*.

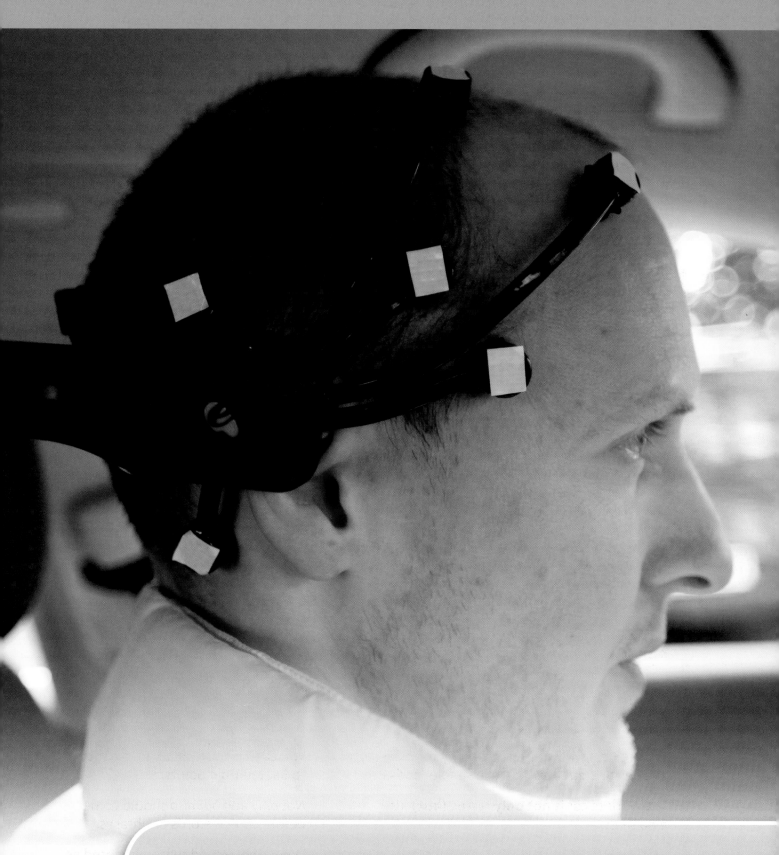

PROJECT

Conduct market research. Research how your invention is different from similar products on the market. From these results, make changes to your invention. Share your new ideas with the class and explain why you made the changes.

Credits

Photo Credits

1 Paul Nicklen/NGC, **3, 56** Gordon Wiltsie/NGC, **4–5, 74** Stephen Alvarez/NGC, **11** Sukree Sukplang/Reuters, **12** (c) Peter Bernik/Shutterstock.com, **13** (tr) Xpacifica/NGC, **13** (cr) Greg Dale/NGC, **14** Pete McBride/NGC, **16** Ken Bohn/Zoological Society of San Diego/Getty Images, **17** Juniors Bildarchiv/F30/Alamy, **18** Design Pics Inc/NGC, **19** Jimmy Chin/NGC, **20–21** (bkgd) Brian J. Skerry/NGC, **21** (br), **113** Gary Burke/Flickr Vision/Getty Images, **22** Handout/Hulton Archive/Getty Images, **24** fivespots/Shutterstock.com, **25** Rick C West-Birdspiders.com, **26** Joel Sartore/NGC, **27, 28–29** Joel Sartore/NGC, **31** Catherine Karnow/NGC, **32** Lynn Johnson/NGC, **33** O. Louis Mazatenta/NGC, **34, 114** (l to r) Li Chaoshu/Shutterstock.com, Glayan/Shutterstock.com, In Green/Shutterstock.com, szefei/Shutterstock.com, **35** David Mercado/Reuters, **36** Rebecca Hale/NGC, **37** Richard Olsenius/NGC, **38** Nir Elias/Reuters, **39** (t) Edward Miller/Hulton Archive/Getty Images, **39** (b) John Greim/LightRocket/Getty Images, **41** (l to r) Zurijeta/Shutterstock.com, Ronald Sumners/Shutterstock.com, Hans Kim/Shutterstock.com, Rehan Qureshi/Shutterstock.com, **42** Rebecca Conway/Reuters, **43** Courtesy of Abid Mehmood, **44** He Lulu/Xinhua Press/Corbis, **45** He Lulu/Xinhua Press/Corbis, **46** Anindito Mukherjee/Reuters, **47, 48–49** Randy Olson/NGC, **51** Andrew H. Brown/NGC, **52** Courtesy of Hayat Sindi, **53** Courtesy of Diagnostics For All, **54** Encyclopaedia Britannica/Universal Images Group/Getty Images, **55** Mudrats Alexandra/ITAR-TASS/Landov, **57** Gordon Wiltsie/NGC, **58** Bennett Raglin/WireImage/Getty Images, **59** Scott S. Warren/NGC, **60** Sarah Leen/NGC, **61** Huguette Roe/Shutterstock.com, **62** Chor Sokunthe/Reuters, **63** zebra0209/Shutterstock.com, **64** Ari N/Shutterstock.com, **65** Joel Sartore/NGC, **66** Simon Rawles/The Image Bank/Getty Images, **67, 68–69** Alexander Hassenstein-FIFA/FIFA/Getty Images, **71** Alison Wright/NGC, **72** (tl) Jonathan Kingston/NGC, **72** (tr) Francois Lenoir/Reuters, **73** (bkgd) Walter Bibikow/Getty Images, **73** (bl) DEA Picture Library/Getty Images, **75** Benoit Tessier/Reuters, **76** Vincenzo Pinto/AFP/Getty Images, **77** Norbert Schiller/Getty Images News/Getty Images, **78** Richard Nowitz/NGC, **79** Bruce Dale/NGC, **80** (t) Maggie Steber/NGC, **80** (br) mikiekwoods/Shutterstock.com, **80** (br) Courtesy of Foldit, **82** James P. Blair/NGC, **83** Daniel Morel/Reuters/Landov, **84** (bkgd) Courtesy of Albert Lin, **84** (br) James L. Stanfield/NGC, **85** Courtesy of Albert Lin, **86** Alison Wright/NGC, **87, 88–89** China Daily/Reuters, **91** Borge Ousland/NGC, **92** Marty Melville/Getty Images, **93** (bl) Joe Brock/Reuters, **93** (br) DCN Diving Group/Barcroft Media/Landov, **94, 125** A. T. Willett/Alamy, **95** Courtesy of Ushahidi Haiti Project (UHP), **96** Joe Scherschel/NGC, **97** Stan Honda/Getty Images, **98** Skip O'Donnell/E+/Getty Images, **99** Jim Richardson/NGC, **100** Brian Snyder/Reuters, **101** Emotiv Lifesciences/NGC, **102** Jodi Cobb/NGC, **103** Karen Bleier/AFP/Getty Images, **104** Sheng Li/Reuters, **105** Toby Melville/Reuters, **106** Yuriko Nakao/Reuters, **107, 108–109** Fabian Bimmer/Reuters, **116** Rebecca Conway/Reuters, **122** Jodi Cobb/NGC, **127** Fabrizio Bensch/Reuters

NGC = National Geographic Creative

Illustration Credits

12–13 (bkgd) Cengage Learning, **56, 92, 94** National Geographic Maps

Text Credits

14 Adapted from "Be Your Best Friend If You'll Be Mine: Alliance Hypothesis For Human Friendship" by the University of Pennsylvania, Science Daily, 5 June 2009: http://www.sciencedaily.com/releases/2009/06/090602204301.htm; **22, 23** Adapted from "Fear Itself" by Sebastian Junger: http://www.nationalgeographic.com/adventure/sebastian-junger/fear-sierra-leone.html; **34, 114** Adapted from "On Beyond 100" by Stephen S. Hall: http://ngm-uat.nationalgeographic.com/archive/on-beyond-100-longevity/; **42, 116** Adapted from "Sayad Gul Kalash: Archaeologist": http://www.nationalgeographic.com/explorers/bios/sayed-gul-kalash/; **52** Adapted from "Hayat Sindi: Science Entrepreneur": http://www.nationalgeographic.com/explorers/bios/hayat-sindi/; **54** Adapted from "Failure is an Option" by Hannah Block: http://ngm-uat.nationalgeographic.com/archive/failure-is-an-option-where-would-we-be-without-it/; **62** Adapted from Wikipedia.com; **74** From "Prince of Prints" by Pat Walters: http://ngm.nationalgeographic.com/125-exploration/risk-takers-gallery#/19; **82** Adapted from "The Genius of Swarms" by Peter Miller: http://ngm.nationalgeographic.com/2007/07/swarms/miller-text; **94** Adapted from "Tornado Survivor Tells Her Story": http://channel.nationalgeographic.com/channel/videos/tornado-survivor-tells-her-story/; **95** Adapted from "Patrick Meier": http://www.nationalgeographic.com/explorers/bios/patrick-meier/ and "Crisis Mapper": http://ngm-beta.nationalgeographic.com/archive/crisis-mapper/; **102** Adapted from "Will Driverless Cars Dominate Our Future?" by Dan Stone: http://newswatch.nationalgeographic.com/2012/11/16/will-driverless-cars-dominate-our-future/